The Big Miss

The Big Miss

How Organizations Overlook the Value of Emotions

Zhecho Dobrev

BUSINESS EXPERT PRESS

Leader in applied, concise business books

First published in 2022 by
Business Expert Press, LLC
222 East 46th Street, New York, NY 10017
www.businessexpertpress.com

ISBN-13: 978-1-63742-256-4 (paperback)
ISBN-13: 978-1-63742-257-1 (e-book)

Business Expert Press Marketing Collection

First edition: 2022

10 9 8 7 6 5 4 3 2 1

Description

In *The Big Miss: How Businesses Overlook the Value of Emotions,* Zhecho Dobrev reveals how organizations are frequently deceived by customers and *fail to act on what they fail to notice*—**thus are missing the biggest driver of profitable customer behavior!** His extensive research shows that emotions are the key drivers of customer behavior, yet few organizations have a strategy to evoke specific emotions based on science and data. Does yours have?

In this book, the author provides business leaders with a *practical framework for how to embed emotions in their business practices,* which includes learning how to:

- Discover the difference between what customers say and do;
- Create a data-based strategy around specific emotions;
- Use customer science to future-proof your business and make the most out of digital transformation, data, and AI;

… and much more.

Keywords

why emotions are key to customer experience management; how businesses can design for emotion and growth; why digital transformation programs fail to deliver results; using data, AI and behavior science in experience design; customer science based strategy for business managers; how to businesses can appeal to customer emotions

Contents

Foreword

"This is business. Leave the emotions at the door." Sounds familiar? I share my own personal story which proved just how wrong this thinking is.

In 2008, Maersk Line was the largest container shipping company in the world. Due to globalization and outsourcing, the industry had seen extraordinary growth and opportunity for decades. However, the financial crisis of 2008 and overcapacity in the industry put Maersk Line into vicious price wars with competitors, resulting in losses and vastly lower margins. The company leadership decided to fight back by building a strategy around differentiation as a premium brand. In support of that strategy, I was asked to lead a global initiative called Customer Experience Innovation.

My first step was to build as diverse a team as I could, representing different cultures, functions, backgrounds, ages, experience, and skills. But once the team was formed, what next? I knew we needed help. I researched several consultancies. One stood out—Beyond Philosophy. They understood B2B; Customer Experience is what they do (vs. general management consultants). The CEO, Colin Shaw, was a clear thought leader in this space and the company had absolutely the best survey mechanism. The survey was called the Emotional Signature, and rather than just getting the usual satisfied/not satisfied, it was designed to uncover the subconscious needs Customers have. I have a master's in statistics and appreciated the elegant and sound design.

Perhaps even more important than the statistics underneath was the simplicity with which the results were provided. It made it abundantly clear where we needed to focus and that became our foundation. Interestingly, the results were almost completely at odds with where most thought we should focus on to improve the customer experience. Rather than service quality, such as on-time delivery, correct invoices, and snazzy websites, the Customers needed us to help them resolve problems, show empathy, and be proactive in our communications. This was about *emotions*. So the saying, "This is business. Leave the emotions at the door" is erroneous and blind to science. As human beings, we experience the world through our senses. And the things that touch our senses drive emotions. Psychology and overwhelming business research show that focusing on emotions is a sound business strategy. The Emotional Signature was the best tool I had to prove this point to the C-suite and our colleagues.

Armed with our focus areas, we selected colleagues from around the world to be our ambassadors. Together, we set out to find ways to make our Customers feel *trust, cared for,* and *happy.* Many of the ideas were simple. Most did not cost a penny more. It was about *how* we did things, as much as what we did. I was absolutely amazed at many creative and innovative ideas from the teams.

The results far exceeded what we imagined could be done. Our Net Promoter Score (NPS) improved by 40 points in two and a half years. We were able to show a direct correlation between improved NPS and the increase in Customers' volume. Perhaps the part I loved the most was the significant improvement in employee engagement. Gone were the days of 1-800-who-cares. Colleagues talked about "my Customers." *Trust, cared for,* and *happy* spilled over in how people worked and treated each other.

If you are thinking of reading the book, my recommendation is YES! That initiative and Beyond Philosophy changed my life. I see the world through different, and I believe, wiser eyes. Do I believe others can do what we did? YES! I plan to with my current company Hellmann Worldwide Logistics. Colin, Zhecho, and the Beyond Philosophy Tteam are already part of my Quality Customer Experience core team.

P.S. You may wonder why the word Customer is capitalized in aforementioned story. During our rollout at Maersk, a colleague shared with me that he decided to capitalize the C in Customers to (1) highlight their significance and (2) remember they are real people. I never forgot that and took that idea with me.

—**Michél Patterson**
North America VP
Digital Transformation and Innovation,
Customer Implementation, and Performance

Introduction

"You guys have religion. I don't. Prove to me that emotions drive value in business." These were the words of an executive of a global insurance provider toward us more than a decade ago when we were talking about focusing on customer emotions. That was and feels like it was a long time ago. Since then, Beyond Philosophy has done research with London Business School proving that in fact emotions do drive value in business and a lot more other organizations have done the same.

Nowadays, it seems like we don't have to convince people that emotions are essential in business. But, and it's a big "but," how many organizations are actually deliberate about evoking certain targeted emotions? How many CEOs have you heard talking to staff about focusing their strategy on making an emotional connection with customers and evoking specific emotions? And that is a big miss because by not being deliberate and not operationalizing the focus on certain emotions, organizations miss on the biggest driver of customer attitudes and behavior.

Hold on, some people might say, we do have data on customer emotions. We are measuring emotions. We have heard this answer many times. But do you? Just very recently, someone working in the research department of a large pharmaceutical company said to us they measure emotions. So when I checked, "so you are measuring the extent to which customers feel trust, feel cared for, feel valued and appreciated," that person said, "No, we don't have that kind of data." Most people we speak to, when they say that they measure emotions, they mean doing some sentiment analysis on customer verbatims. That could indeed be useful if done using a trained Machine Learning (ML) algorithm, as we'll discuss in the later chapters of the book, but then again, that's not what most organizations are doing.

Hold on a minute, you still might say. We may not be explicitly measuring those, but our executives are intelligent people, they know what customers want. The fact is that customers themselves don't know what they really want and what really drives their behavior. We'll explain the underlying psychological reasons for this phenomenon later in the book but just consider some of these examples. The premium customers of a charge card company said the most important thing for them was that the card is accepted by more merchants. The company's executives would often say that this is the big elephant in the room. However, it turned out that it was the feeling of prestige that was really driving their engagement with the company. Telecom customers in both the United States and the Middle East would say that the most important for them was the network when, in fact, it was how customers felt about the organization that was making them renew their contracts. How do we know? Because we have done research with organizations in those sectors. Just like we've done research with a global U.S. earth-moving equipment manufacturer, whose customers said they wanted dependable machines and available parts for maintenance but then again it was them feeling cared for and respected as customers that made them buy again from the manufacturer. Or how about patients of a U.S. hospital system saying the most important for them is to spend more time with the doctor, when in fact it was not the quantity of time spent with the doctor but the quality of the interaction during that time. It was their silent need to feel genuinely listened to and empathized with that really affected the patient's perception and made them recommend the hospital system to others. A great deal of the manner in which people act on the surface is driven by subconscious aspects and emotions of which they are not necessarily aware of.

No wonder many customer experience programs fail to deliver the desired results. Imagine going to your chief financial officer (CFO) and saying we need to lower our rates because to improve customer satisfaction we need to make the card accepted by more merchants. Or walking out to the CFO and saying we need to either bring in more general practitioners (GPs) or plan for fewer time slots within their schedule so they can spend more time with the patients. You'd lose your job either right at the moment or a few months later when it turns out the whole thing was a deception and it's not what customers really wanted.

"I think because, at the end of the day, what consumers told us they would do, and what they actually did, were different things," says Simon Fox, the chief executive of the publisher behind the launch of a new newspaper called *New Day*. It closed less than three months after it was launched! [1] It was released on the basis of market research that showed readers wanted a positive, politically neutral newspaper.

"'We underestimated the deep emotional bond' they [the most loyal customers] had with the original packaging," says Neil Campbell, president at Tropicana North America, part of PepsiCo Americas Beverages, after a packaging redesign led to a 20 percent drop in sales for the famous orange juice in North America. This meant a loss of $30M of revenue, not to mention the investment of $35M for an advertising campaign to accompany the package redesign. [2] "What we didn't get was the passion this very loyal small group of consumers have. That wasn't something that came out in the research," he goes on to add.

These two stories go on to show not just the dangers of getting customer research wrong and being deceived by what customers say they want but also the power of customer emotional bonds and the unconscious drivers of customer behavior. To understand why customers behave the way they do, you need to understand how our minds are made to work and the role emotions play in decision making.

How the world perceives the role emotions play in decision making started to change with the work of Antonio Damasio and his wife. The pair spent decades studying people who had suffered brain injuries resulting in their emotions being impaired but whose reason was otherwise unaffected. They discovered that those people found it really hard to make decisions and that emotions play a central role in decision making. Their insights date back to the early 1990s; Colin Shaw's book, *The DNA of Customer Experience: How Emotions Drive Value* (Palgrave MacMillan), was published in 2007; we met the first large organization that actually measures emotions in 2013, but to date, we have rarely seen an organization taking a systematic approach to evoking and measuring emotions...

Fast forward to the present time. Many organizations have invested millions or billions of dollars in customer experience programs, hired customer experience specialists and chief customer officers, implemented measurement programs... Yet customer experience indexes are stagnating or are in retreat mode; high street retailers are defaulting. Only that it doesn't have to be this way. There is plenty of evidence that organizations can reap the benefits of their customer experience programs, and retailers that master an emotional connection with customers flourish and grow.

After a long research on our large database covering nine industry sectors and a multitude of organizations from the United States, the United Kingdom, Europe, Middle East, Africa, and Asia, we found that businesses miss on the biggest driver of value (i.e., profitable customer behavior). It is not showing on their radars because many organizations use flawed research methods (i.e., relying heavily on what customers say they want, etc.) or they don't include emotions in their research and predictive analytics. By not doing so, they miss 50 percent of the picture! Consequently, by not being deliberate about creating an emotional attachment with customers, most of the time, they waste resources focusing on less impactful or outright deceptive aspects.

Take as an example the plastic debit and credit cards. You've had dozens or even over 100 of them, right? And you've chopped all but a handful of them, never feeling that you are losing something, right? But then I remember when Barclays came up with a feature allowing you to customize it with a picture of your choice. I printed it with a picture of my relatively new girlfriend at the time (now my partner and mother of my son). I was in a distant relationship with her at the time, and when I showed her the card, I said, "now I can't take another girl out and pay for dinner" (which was, of course, not true as I had several other credit cards, but still…). I could see that this created positive emotions in her and had a very deep emotional impact. She took it as a sign that I'm serious about the relationship. Later, when I'd go to the pub, I'd see other people with Barclays credit cards, waiting to order, who had their pets, and so on, on the cards, and once or twice we had a good laugh about it. Clearly, the technology and logistics came at a cost to Barclays, but they must have realized that this will create an emotional attachment to something as lame as a plastic card, and when the time came to get it scrapped, people would feel they are losing something. I know because when Barclays had to reissue my card with a different sort-code on it, my first and only question was, "It'll be with the same picture, right?"

While on the subject of cards, I remember an article in *Bloomberg* about the time JP Morgan Chase made a card with a weighty metal core (i.e., the Chase Sapphire Reserve card). It was in such high demand that in just three weeks, Chase burned through its inventory of metal card stock that was supposed to last 10 to 12 months. Yes, Chase had designed a good product in terms of bonus points, and so on, but for a $450 annual fee, they had to get something else right to create fans, not just customers. Here's what a customer said, "I have the Chase Sapphire Preferred, and virtually nothing gives me more pleasure when I pay and the cashier notices how gorgeous that card is." [3]

Now tell me, where is the rational thinking in that? It's all about the emotion! Of course, this was no news to us as we knew for a long time that American Express Centurion customers, whose card is made of titanium, feel the same way. The card weighs more, feels different and cool when you touch it, and gives the feeling of prestige to customers. A psychological explanation could be that, according to experiential psychology, we associate weight with importance. From an early age, we learn that it takes a lot more energy to move heavier objects and therefore we only spend energy on worthwhile activities. An experiment by University of Amsterdam psychologist Nils Jostmann and his colleagues even showed that carrying a heavier clipboard, rather than a light one, changes people's perception and the value they associate to things. [4] They found that those who carried heavier clipboards overestimated the value of various foreign currencies, so next time you go for a job interview, you may want to put your CV on a clipboard! It may also be that the weight raises customers' dopamine levels. According to Sean McQuay, the credit card expert at NerdWallet, "Chase has basically realized that the weight raises customers' dopamine levels." [5] Dopamine is a hormone associated with the brain's reward system and pleasurable sensations (in later chapters we'll reveal more academic research on the link between certain hormones, emotions, and behavior). Given all this, at present times, it comes as no surprise to us to see that most of the fastest growing FinTech companies offer the option of a premium metal card. [6] Yet, many established financial organizations missed on this.

Here is the conundrum though: as we've said earlier, if you ask credit card customers what they want, they're most likely to tell you they want rational things such as low interest rates, more points, cashback, and the cards to be accepted by more merchants. (It's logical, isn't it? When the card is not accepted, there is not much use for it!)

We will review this phenomenon and the underlying psychological reasons for it in the book and we'll reveal previously unpublished research on the extent to which the various customer life cycle touchpoints that businesses typically measure drive business value across different industries and why businesses are missing on the key driver of value ($$$).

We'll provide further evidence from other researchers and explain our research findings through the works of notorious academics: Nobel Laureates for economics, professors of psychology, and marketing.

We'll discuss what this means when it comes to managing the customer experience in an organization and the reasons why it's stagnating. Heads up—this is huge and requires a fundamental shift, not just in understanding but in action. Because, if businesses were focused when making decisions on what would foster an emotional connection, they would make different decisions. But we know that they are not. And they are about to miss the boat big time as they are now busy designing digital experiences as if they are a process of clicks. We also know that it is not working well either because reports say that about 70 percent of digital transformation projects fail to deliver the results they envisaged. That puts the wastage figure at about $900 billion annually. [7]

We'll also show how the brand and marketing can foster an emotional connection with customers at a time of a generational shift.

Finally, we'll build a picture of how customer experience management will look in the new digital world post-Covid-19 with the rise of customer science teams and AI-powered data analysis.

PART I

What Do Organizations Miss on Today?

Consumers don't think about how they feel. They don't say what they think and they don't do what they say

—David Ogilvy

Colin Shaw, the CEO of Beyond Philosophy LLC and author of seven best-selling books on the topic of customer experience, always thought that we have been sitting on a gold mine. We had gathered a large database of millions of data points related to the various aspects of customer experience, 20 emotions, and proxies for future financial performance for organizations. It's been so large that we just couldn't get our heads around it on how to proceed about analyzing it. Just as it so often happens, when you have a problem in the back of your mind, one day you look at it from another angle and the solution hits you in the face. As all our client engagements got put on a temporary hold in the midst of the Covid-19 pandemic, I went on to analyze a large part of our database with some nagging questions in mind. In Chapter 1, "The Nagging Questions," we'll explain what those are and provide some background on prior research into the role of emotions in business. Notably, the question that put me on the path of this research was finding how important the feeling of a relationship with an organization actually is in comparison to product quality, price, ease of use, customer service, account management, the digital self-service capabilities, and so on.

In Chapter 2, "*Big* Research Findings," we will explain our methodology and the main findings of our research. After analyzing a vast amount of data from many large organizations in nine different industries across the United States and Canada, the United Kingdom, and the rest of the world, we found that the feeling of relationship and the overall emotional attachment to an organization are much bigger drivers of value compared to the traditional touchpoints that organizations look at. However, those typically do not feature on their journey maps, organizations don't measure them, and they don't have a deliberate strategy for how to go about them. Therein lies a big miss and a big opportunity for organizations.

Our research also found that customers themselves don't know what they really want and that could be the reason why these emotional attachment aspects seldom get registered on organizations' radars. In addition, not measuring emotions could leave organizations blind for a big part of the experience as our research also revealed that emotions account for almost 50 percent of value in the experience.

Don't just take our word for it, though. In Chapter 3, "Evidence From Independent Research," we will look at the research other organizations have made about the role of emotions in customer experience and business. It also turned out that academic research shows that what makes customers buy more from organizations are largely the same things that make patients rate their physicians and hospital stay higher and also what makes some personal partner relationships endure while others fail.

Why is it that emotional aspects play such an important role and yet, when you ask people, they say that other things are a lot more important? In Chapter 4, "The Psychological Explanation," we will try to answer this question by looking at how our brains are made to function. We will share fascinating discoveries from highly esteemed psychologists and academics. So let's get on to it...

CHAPTER 1

The Nagging Questions

Hands up if you think relationships are important in business! Every time we ask this question, we see a forest of hands up in the air. But exactly how important are relationships when you compare them to product quality, price, ease of use, customer service, account management, or self-service capabilities? We set on several-month-long research to find out the answer to this and other nagging questions ... but first some background.

Antonio Damasio's Research

For most of 20th century, the predominant thinking was that people are mostly rational and make sound decisions. At the same time, emotions such as fear, hatred, or affection were seen as the reasons why people deviate from rationality. As such, emotions were deemed not to have a role in the business world.

This was about to change when neuroscientist Antonio Damasio met a patient named Elliot. Elliot had been a good husband, father, and successful businessman. Soon after he started to suffer from severe headaches and become easily distracted at work, his doctors found a tumor in his brain, almost the size of a baseball. The doctors carefully removed the tumor from the brain, but relatives quickly discovered that Elliot was no longer the same. His intelligence and speech were intact, but often he couldn't even make routine decisions. Having to organize his documents at work, he couldn't decide whether to sort them by date, size, or relevance to the case, while choosing where to have lunch took all afternoon. Despite being made aware of this flow and the time he was losing, he could not correct it. A brain scan showed that his IQ, memory, and learning capabilities were fine, but when they started testing his emotional capability with images of injured people and burning houses, it was revealed that he couldn't feel anything.

Elliot dispassionately reported to Damasio that his life was falling apart. While still in the 97th percentile for IQ, his marriage collapsed, as did each new business he started. Damasio found Elliott an "uninvolved spectator" in his own life. In his book *Descartes' Error: Emotion, Reason and the Human Brain* (first published in 1994), Damasio writes:

> He was always controlled. Nowhere was there a sense of his own suffering, even though he was the protagonist. I never saw a tinge of emotion in my many hours of conversation with him: no sadness, no impatience, no frustration. [1]

Damasio and his wife, Hanna Damasio, had since spent years working with patients, who had suffered brain injuries resulting in their emotions being impaired, but whose reason was otherwise unaffected. They found time and time again that these people were perfectly capable of reason and leading a conversation, but when it came to making a decision, that is, should I eat chicken or pasta, they couldn't come up with one. The advancement of technology meant that they could use imaging techniques such as magnetic resonance imaging (MRI) to study patients and start understanding more about the areas of the brain involved in different types of emotion.

The work of Antonio Damasio completely debunked the myth that emotions have no role in decision making (or that they must be kept out). It turned out that emotions were central for moving a thinking human being to take action.

Here is the main point, though. In the preface to the 2005 edition of *Descartes Error*, Damasio wrote,

> Today this idea [that emotion assists the reasoning process] does not cause any raised eyebrows. However, while this idea may not raise any eyebrows today among neuroscientists, I believe it's still a surprise to the general public. We're trained to regard emotions as irrational impulses that are likely to lead us astray. [2]

More than 20 years into the 21st century, my observations show that businesses have still not fully come to grasp this concept and have not really operationalized creating emotions while conducting business. If you think about it, the average age of the board of directors of the S&P 500 companies for 2017 was 62.4 years. [3] That means that most board members have been educated based on the idea that emotions derail sound decision making, not that they facilitate it, as an abundance of subsequent work and the new field of behavioral science have shown. And because most organizations are not measuring emotions, their analysis can't pinpoint them as something to focus on and thus those are missed by organizations' radars.

Jason Ten-Pow, author of *UNBREAKABLE: A Proven Process for Building Unbreakable Relationships With Customers*, thinks that since the 2008 financial crisis, executives have focused on cost-cutting and automation and have largely neglected making any methodological steps toward creating deeper, more emotional relationships with customers. [4] So whether it's because of how they were taught when growing up, whether it's due to their methods of research, or whether it's because of their focus on costs and automation, there is overwhelming evidence that most businesses are not being deliberate in focusing on creating emotional relationships with customers and this is a big missed opportunity.

Beyond Philosophy's 2005 to 2007 Research

When the second edition of *Descartes Error* was published (2005), Beyond Philosophy, a pioneering customer experience consultancy selected by the *Financial Times* as being one of the leading management consultancies for four years in a row and counting (and where I've been working as a management consultant for the last 12+ years), received a challenge from a German executive of an insurer, with operations across the globe, to prove to him that emotions are indeed important in business as the team has been saying and that emotions affect business value. "The challenge with you guys is that you have religion, you believe in this, but I don't have a religion. Prove to me that emotions drive value in business," he said. So, Beyond Philosophy set on a two-year-long research with professors from London Business School. The research culminated in Colin Shaw's book, *The DNA of Customer Experience: How Emotions Drive Value*, Palgrave Macmillan, 2007. The team found 20 emotions (12

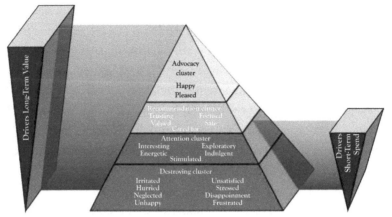

Figure 1.1 Beyond Philosophy's 20 emotions that drive and destroy value

positive and 8 negative) that drive and destroy business value and we have been measuring them with organizations ever since.

The original research (Figure 1.1) found four clusters of emotions: the Advocacy cluster consisting of happy and pleased; the Recommendation cluster with trusting, valued, focused, safe, and cared for; the Attention cluster with interesting, energetic, stimulated, pampered (indulgent), and exploring options (exploratory); and the Destroying cluster with eight negative emotions: disappointed, dissatisfied, irritated, frustrated, neglected, stressed, unhappy, and hurried.

Soon after we started measuring these with clients, we also realized that we need to measure the stimulus for these emotions, that is, the aspects of the experience that evoke those emotions and affect business value.

The Research Objectives

Fast forward to the Covid-19 lockdown in 2020. We have amassed a large database of questions on the various aspects of customer experience that cover all the life cycle stages of the customer journey. In addition, we also have one of the largest databases on emotions and could link all these (the aspects of the experience and the emotions) to business value (i.e., likelihood to recommend the organization, remain a customer, and so on). We have asked over 1M+ questions to customers of some of the largest and most renowned companies across the globe, spanning many different industries.

We've also been working on many Behavioral Journey Mapping (as we call it) projects, and we know that typically organizations look at the customer journey life cycle. A simple Google image search will show you many customer journey life cycle wheels or infinity wheels similar to the one in Figure 1.2.

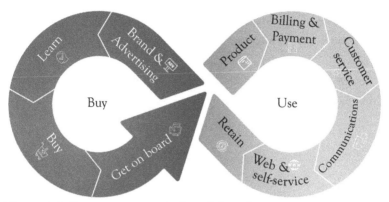

Figure 1.2 Customer journey infinity life cycle

The work from Antonio Damasio and his wife showed that emotions are intrinsic to our decision making. Colin Shaw and Beyond Philosophy have proven that emotions drive value in business. Still though, sitting in the lockdown, we had some nagging questions:

- Which of the customer journey life cycle moments drive the most business value?
- Is there something important that these customer journey wheels are missing, that is, where is the place to consider how organizations create the feeling of a relationship with their customers and form an emotional attachment?
- How vital is actually the feeling of a relationship and the emotional attachment compared to the other customer journey lifecycle moments such as the buying experience, the product experience, the digital self-service experience, the customer service experience, the communications they receive from organizations, and the rest of the customer life cycle journey moments?

- What journey moments have the biggest influence on the feeling of a relationship with the organization?
- What role do emotions play compared to the rational aspects of the experience?
- Is there a difference between what customers say they want and what really drives business value ($$$)?
- Is there a big difference between business-to-business (B2B) and business-to-consumer (B2C) or between industries?

So we set out on a research mission to provide quantifiable answers to these questions.

CHAPTER 2

Big Research Findings

Research Framework

Someone said that our best work is the work we find ourselves doing when there is no obligation to do so. When Covid-19 put on hold our projects I found myself with a bit of time on my hands and those nagging questions in mind. So I rolled up my sleeves to do a substantial research with 18,537 customers of 24 large organizations (all of which are well-known organizations within their sectors and almost all are publicly listed companies) from 9 different industry sectors, analyzing 59 customer groups. Eighty percent of the respondents were in the United States and Canada, 8 percent were in the United Kingdom, and 12 percent were from the rest of the world (primarily the Middle East and South-East Asia). While just 29 percent of the respondents were from the B2B sector, almost half the models (customer groups) we analyzed (46 percent) were B2B.

What do we mean by a "model"?

We find what drives business value by using predictive analytics. We construct a Structural Equation Model, based on data from a customer survey, where customers have answered questions about 40 or so aspects of their experience with a company (*the stimuli*), to what extent they feel the 20 emotions (Figure 1.1) that we know to drive or destroy business value (*the response*), and questions relating to business value (*the effect*). The framework of our model (Figure 1.2) follows the rationale of "stimulus–response–effect," that is, through all the things the organization does (e.g., the various aspects of its customer experience, grouped in customer life cycle touchpoint categories) it stimulates the customer one way or another. This in turn creates positive or negative emotions and all these things (the aspects of the experience and the emotions) affect the customer attitudes and behavior toward the organization (i.e., business value for the organization; Figure 2.1).

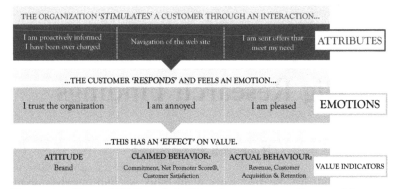

Figure 2.1 Beyond Philosophy's Stimulus-response-effect model

Each model is with a distinct customer group (segment). So, for example, with one insurer we had personal (B2C) and commercial (B2B) customer models; with one mobile telecom we had premium customers, budget customers, large enterprise, and small enterprise (two B2C and two B2B models); with a large equipment manufacturer we analyzed four models based on geography (North America, South America, Europe, and Asia-Pacific) and a number based on the size of the customer business (i.e., small enterprises, medium, and large enterprises), and so on.

What do we mean by "value"? Customers generate value for businesses mainly by (continuing) using their products and services and by spreading the word about them. In addition to that, truly engaged customers are also willing to pay more or travel further just to purchase/use an organization's products and services, and then there's the brand halo effect, that is, customers will be willing to purchase additional/different categories of products and services from the same company. To measure whether customers are likely to bring value to organizations, over time a number of proxy metrics have been developed. In our particular case and research, when we say value, we mean proxies for future financial performance and business growth such as:

- *Likelihood to recommend* (the question that measures the Net Promoter Score (NPS®)[1]—a known proxy for business growth)
- *Retention*—likelihood to renew subscription/policy or remain a customer (a proxy for retaining existing customers)
- *Ease of doing business/customer effort score* (CES; another known proxy for customer loyalty and business growth)
- *Preference over the competition* (a proxy for brand differentiation and true customer loyalty as opposed to convenience)

Now, from here onwards, when we say that something drives value, we mean the aggregate of all of these "value indicators." Combining these metrics gives us several advantages. We are combining a customer advocacy question (likelihood to recommend), which could be a predictor of new customer growth (especially if the score is higher than that of competitors) with a retention question, which is a predictor of future churn rate. To that, we also add the CES/ease of doing business, which some argue is an even more accurate predictor of growth than NPS®. [1] This way we don't need to take sides in the debate about which metric is best. Joke apart, I read somewhere (unfortunately I can't remember where I read it) that "basket metrics" (such as this combination) trumps single metrics as a better predictor of company performance. And since we look at many different industries and organizations it makes sense to use a variety of metrics. To the three metrics, mentioned earlier, we add a fourth metric, which measures the degree of brand and offering differentiation. Many of our clients have been interested to learn to what extent customers see them as providing a unique value compared to competitors and how to increase this perception. I remember a story from a former client, that one of the things that set them on the road to become the #1 builder in their market was hearing from a customer that they are not

---

[1] Net Promoter®, NPS®, NPS Prism®, and the NPS-related emoticons are registered trademarks of Bain & Company, Inc., Satmetrix Systems, Inc., and Fred Reichheld. Net Promoter Score® and Net Promoter System® are service marks of Bain & Company, Inc., Satmetrix Systems, Inc., and Fred Reichheld."

worse than any of the other guys. They said to themselves: "Is this what we want to be known for?" A U.S. shipping company, when measuring customer attachment, was also asking whether customers were willing to drive five more miles just to get to their office. This way, you can get to the true customer sentiment and not just usage by convenience.

There have been many studies and statistics on the value of customer experience, but still, some business executives do challenge the linkage between these metrics and real-world company performance. In our experience, there are several reasons for this. To begin with, how things correlate when analyzing two variables on the same 0 to 10/1 to 5 scale will inevitably be higher than in the real world when all the complexities are considered. In the real world, you have all the various product and experience aspects, all the memories from using the organization, the perception of competitors, the habits of using an organization (how many organizations do you use just out of habit or convenience despite not being particularly happy with their services), and the perceived switching costs, however small they may appear to be. For example, when you consider switching to another business bank account, while it's quite easy to just open another bank account, you then have to get used to the new layout of the mobile and web banking (not so difficult you'd think); you'll incur some costs from moving your money from one bank to another but the worse, in my opinion, is that you'll lose all your saved payees (so you'll have to manually enter them all over again). Then, there could be fears that you'll have to inform all those who do pay you money that you've changed your bank account and hope that they'll remember to send the money to your new bank account (you can take this as an example of the behavioral science principle called "loss aversion," which basically states that people hate losing much more than they like winning and the ratio is roughly 2.5 to 1, but we'll talk more about behavioral science in the next chapters). So, understandably, an incremental increase in customer metrics may not immediately bring you a whole lot of benefits. Besides, to assess your experience, you should not just look at how customers rate you, but where you stack versus your competitors and whether the market is expanding or shrinking.

Consequently, to prove the financial benefits you often need to achieve substantial movement in the key performance indicator (KPI) metrics. I remember speaking, many years ago, to the global head of the NPS® program for Vodafone. NPS®, as introduced with the infamous 2006 book of Fred Reichheld, *The Ultimate Question: Driving Good Profits and True Growth*," basically asks the question "How likely are you to recommend the organization to a friend, colleague or relative?" You can then take the percentage of customers who answered the question with 9 and 10, called promoters, and subtract the percentage of customers who gave you a rating between zero and six, as they are called detractors, and you'll get to your organization's NPS®. I won't go into any more detail about that because there have been scores of literature devoted to its application and the surrounding controversy. The Vodafone contact was in charge of the program in 25 different countries and we had a discussion about customer experience metrics. He told me that before they used the TRI*M system (which about 12 years ago involved measuring the perceived performance on aspects of the experience and their importance to customers thus coming up with a metric), then moved to customer satisfaction, then moved to NPS, and at the time of our conversation they were contemplating on changing their key metric yet again because they couldn't move the needle.

Then, you also need to be measuring and tracking operational performance as well as the various aspects of the actual customer experience at the same cadence as your customer experience KPIs, to be able to do the linkage. We have seen many organizations plunge in customer experience and journey mapping projects, which are then unable to prove any benefits because they were not tracking operational and experience metrics to begin with.

But, above all, to affect change in the metrics, an organization needs to find first what actually drives the metrics and take action on it. This is the difference between what we call customer outcome metrics (commonly used customer experience KPIs such as NPS, customer satisfaction (CSAT), etc.) and customer experience metrics (i.e., different aspects of the experience your customers had; Figure 2.2).

To illustrate the difference, I'll use an analogy I heard from a speaker at a customer experience conference in Kiev, Ukraine. He really had grabbed the crowd. To give you an idea about the emotions of the attendees, I'll create a spectrum for you. Before I spoke, the lecturer was a professor

Customer Experience (CX) Metrics vs Customer Outcome (CO) Metrics

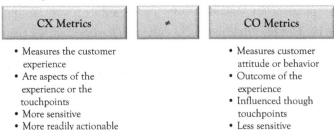

CX Metrics	≠	CO Metrics
• Measures the customer experience • Are aspects of the experience or the touchpoints • More sensitive • More readily actionable		• Measures customer attitude or behavior • Outcome of the experience • Influenced though touchpoints • Less sensitive

Figure 2.2 Customer experience versus customer outcome metrics

from a Swiss university who spoke about Big Data. While clearly knowledgeable, he had too much of a focus on science and less on the emotional appeal (i.e., storytelling): his slides were black and white, mostly with formulas and bullet points. So it was no surprise the audience was mostly bored and about to fall asleep, while I was trying to keep up as I found the topic interesting. I'll put him at one end of the spectrum. Me, on the other hand, thinking about the experience of conference attendees, who sit for the best part of a day, listening to people, who think they know it all, I tried to instill humor and stories in between the important learning points. I thought I'd done quite well considering the laugh and the response from the attendees. However, that was till the last speaker started. The organizers had purposefully left him at the end (we'll talk about the behavioral science principle called the peak–end rule later on) because he had been voted the best speaker at their previous conference. And I could see why! His "presentation" consisted of drawing a bird on a flip-chart paper and some dots to indicate the bird's poo. He spent the entire time telling stories and referring to that drawing. He was speaking to the Ukrainian attendees in their native language and using the translation services. I couldn't understand it, but the audience was having the laugh of their lives and one couldn't help but notice that it erupted every time he mentioned the word "poo" or "sh*t." His main point was this: focusing on the NPS number is like focusing on the bird's poop. If you want to affect the outcome (i.e., what the poop looks like) you have to affect what goes in the bird's digestive system. Similarly, if your child gets a D on math, to affect the outcome, you shouldn't be focusing on the mark itself but on the aspects that affect the outcome, that is, how much time did your child spend studying, how much time you spend with them, the quality of the teacher's explanation, teaching methods, and so on.

This is something that many businesses have been guilty of. It's not so hard to see that, if you only use a one-, two-, or three-question survey (or a three-button happy–unhappy smiley terminal) then you may lack the information necessary to find what really drives these metrics. This is what we tried to find with our research: Which of the typical customer life cycle journey touchpoints drive the most value and how do the relationships and emotions stack up against those? To finish off the topic about linking up these measures to business performance, one of our clients, Maersk Line, the world's largest container shipping company, who went along the way we described, that is, finding what affects the key metric, redesigning that experience to effect change, and tracking both customer and organizational metrics along the way, found that for every 4 percentage points increase in NPS, they get an additional 1 percent in cargo volume. As we said earlier, you need a substantial increase in the metric to be able to calculate the effect and theirs was more than substantial—40 percentage points increase in NPS over 30 months (equating to 10 percent additional shipping volume). This remarkable achievement prompted Forrester to do a case study on their turnaround transformation. [2]

It is therefore important to find the key experience metrics that affect the outcome metrics. Table 2.1 presents the customer life cycle touchpoints that we analyzed in our study and the typical attributes of the experience that form the touchpoint.

The *Big* Findings

Emotional Attachment Is the Biggest Driver of Value

Based on the analysis of the 59 customer groups (46 percent of which are B2B) via predictive analytics we found that "Emotional attachment" is by far the most value-driving factor of the experience. It was the biggest driver of value in 59 percent of the customer groups we analyzed and overall was responsible for 43 percent of business value, more than twice as much as the second ranked "Product and usage" with 20 percent and third ranked "Brand & advertising" with 18 percent.

Table 2.1 Customer life cycle journey touchpoints

Customer life cycle touchpoint	Get onboard	Product/use	Billing & payment
Definition (*i.e., the guiding criteria that we used to assign attributes to that touchpoint*)	All aspects related to the brand perception and advertising	All aspects related to learning more about the product/ service before you buy	All experience aspects related to the purchase of product/ service
Example of attributes	"Acts in socially responsible ways," "Is a brand that I can relate to," "Is a well-known brand," and so on	"Ease of under-standing how plans/costs compare between carriers," "Ease of finding the product information you need," and so on	"Sales Rep made me feel in control of the decision," "Speed of application approval," and so on

Customer life cycle touchpoint	Get onboard	Product/use	Billing & payment
Definition (*i.e., the guiding criteria that we used to assign attributes to that touchpoint*)	All experience aspects related to starting to use the product/service	All aspects related to the product/ service features and price	All aspects related to the billing and payment for products/ services
Example of attributes	"Wait time to receive my machine," "Quality of training," "Speed of installation," and so on	"Competitiveness of price," "Speed of Internet," "Prod-ucts are depend-able," and so on	"Accuracy of invoic-ing," "Payment terms were thoroughly explained," and so on

Customer life cycle touchpoint	Web and self-service	Customer service	Communications
Definition (*i.e., the guiding criteria that we used to assign attributes to that touchpoint*)	All aspects related to web account management, app experience, or digital self-service	All aspects related to customer ser-vices (call center, issue resolutions, etc.)	All aspects related to customer communi-cations

(Continued)

Table 2.1 (Continued)

Example of attributes	"Usefulness of app," "Ability to manage my account online," and so on	"Knowledge of call center representatives," "Speed of problem resolution," "Ease of contacting the company," and so on	"Relevance of communications sent to me," "Receive pro-active notifications," and so on

Customer life cycle touchpoint	Retain	Emotional attachment	
Definition (*i.e., the guiding criteria that we used to assign attributes to that touchpoint*)	All aspects related to contract renewal or activities toward retaining customers	All aspects related to the emotional feeling of a bond and relationship	
Example of attributes	"Recognizing my tenure at the time of contract renewal," "Attrac-tive loyalty pro-grams," and so on	"I feel like I have a relationship with (name of company)," "Listens to me," "I feel appreciated as a customer," and so on	

Now onto the results!

Table 2.2 B2B versus B2C results

Touchpoint category	B2B	B2C
Emotional attachment	48%	40%
Product & use	20%	20%
Brand & advertising	13%	21%
Customer service	4%	13%
Communications	4%	2%
Billing & payment	5%	1%
Buy	3%	2%
Learn	0%	3%
Retain	2%	0%
Get onboard & training	2%	0%
Web & self-service	−2%	−1%

Interestingly, the results showed that "Emotional attachment" is an even bigger driver in B2B with 48 percent compared to 40 percent in B2C (Table 2.2). The probable explanation for this is that in the B2B universe typically there are fewer larger customers, which allows for a more personal and flexible approach, facilitated in many instances by account managers compared to the B2C market, where through mass advertising the brand plays a much bigger role (i.e., it drives 21 percent of business value in B2C vs. 13 percent in B2B). You can also say that the stakes in the B2B market are higher than in B2C and one needs a reliable partner. For example, buying a costly fleet of machines or trusting the entire enterprise communications to a provider might prove a much more costly mistake compared to buying a phone or renewing a car insurance policy.

Another interesting difference is that "Customer service" contributes a lot more value in B2C (large volume of calls to the contact center, large foot traffic to branches) versus B2B, where a large part of issues are handled by account managers and direct contacts. On the other side, "Communications" and especially "Billing & payment" drive more value in the B2B sector. This again makes sense as, typically, billing is much more complex in the B2B where oftentimes service providers are unable to combine multiple client bills into one. It's important to remember that these are aggregate scores across all the models and organizations that we analyzed. So, for example, "Get onboard & training" appears second to bottom from the chart with just 2 percent of the overall value but for a health care software application provider it was the second most value-driving touchpoint of the experience.

When we showed these results to a client we were working with, they were really puzzled by what's on the bottom of the table, that is, the fact that "Web & self-service" destroys value despite all the investment, efforts, and attention that go into that area. In Chapter 12 we will talk about the various reasons why digital transformation projects fail to deliver results and improve the customer experience, but here we would just mention a few things. To begin with, most organizations focus on the digital self-service channels with the idea to automate things and save costs, not really to provide an outstanding experience. Then, in many instances, either the experience failed to meet customer expectations about what they can do online, how intuitive and personalized it should be, and so on, or it was just on par with customer expectations. Finally, what customers do online may be just completing functional tasks, while it is the overall feeling about the company that makes them stick with it or recommend it. For example, in the model of a fully digital personal savings provider, it was the feeling of a relationship with the organization and feeling safe and secure about banking that were the biggest drivers of value rather than the ease of log-in and managing their account through mobile devices. In the case of a B2B health management software application provider, it was whether the customer felt the organization listened to their concerns that had the biggest impact on business value rather than any feature of the application. Later in the book, we will share a report from Forrester with the finding that experiential value is a more important value dimension for customers than functional value. In Chapter 4 we will also provide a psychological explanation about why emotions turn out to be so important when it comes to deciding whether to stick with or recommend an organization. This is not to say that organizations shouldn't invest in the digital experience but that when doing so they should think about how to elicit the key value-driving emotional aspects. We will discuss how to go about doing that in the next chapters and in Part III of the book.

What do we mean by "Emotional attachment"? As with all of the touchpoints in our research, this is a label we gave that amalgamates different aspects of the experience which vary for the different industries and sectors but there is a degree of commonality as well. Initially, we called it "the feeling of a relationship" with the organization, as when we first started thinking about this research we wanted to quantify how important the feeling of a relationship actually is compared to other aspects such as product, customer service, and digital self-service channels. When we had done research with our clients this was oftentimes the #1 driver of value. However, later, when we looked at the other aspects that were lumped together with it, we found that what it comes down to most of the time, other than indeed the feeling of relationship or being recognized as a loyal member/frequent customer, is also about feeling cared for as an individual, feeling valued and appreciated as a customer, the trustworthiness and responsiveness of the organization, feeling respected, being listened to, and so on (Table 2.3).

When you look at these you see that it's beyond just the feeling of a relationship but also about an emotional connection and attachment

Table 2.3 Emotional attachment attributes

Emotional attachment attributes
Cares about me as a person
Values me as a customer
Is trustworthy
I feel like I have a relationship with
Is responsive
Respects me
Listens to me

with the organization. When you think about it, isn't this what our personal relationships are—an emotional attachment. Think about your loved ones, your partner, your parents, your kids: what makes them stand out from the rest of your acquaintances is your emotional attachment to them. We, therefore, decided to relabel the grouping to "Emotional attachment."

Customers Don't Know What They Really Want

Unequivocally, what customers tell you and what they do can be very different. In our research, we found that customers don't know what they really want.

When we do research with clients to find what customers want most, we use a form of conjoint exercise, which allows us to distinguish between "nice to have" and the really important aspects of the experience. The trouble with asking customers to rate the importance of a long list of product and experience attributes on a scale of 0 to 10 is that customers are likely to rate everything with 9 and 10, that is, everything is important to them. So we use an exercise that requires customers to make a series of explicit trade-offs enabling us to identify the relative importance of each attribute by the number of times customers select it as their most or least important consideration (Figure 2.3).

So we use that exercise to find out what customers (say they) want and, as we said earlier, we use predictive analytics (structural equation modeling (SEM)) to find the key drivers of business value (customer attitudes). This way we found that in 74 percent of the customer groups we analyzed, customers state a product-related aspect as the most important for them but in reality, "Product & use" drives the most value only in

How we find...

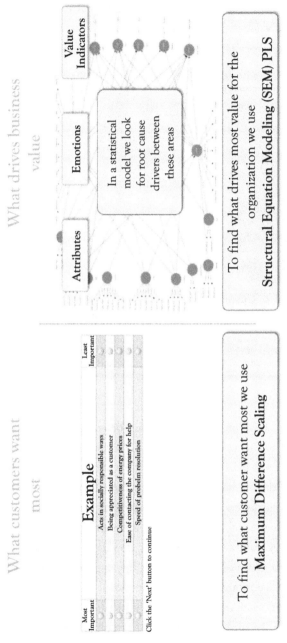

Figure 2.3 How we find what customers want most versus what drives business value

14 percent of the models (customer groups). On the other hand, only 2 percent of the customer groups state an "Emotional attachment" aspect as the most important, when in fact, "Emotional attachment" is the biggest driver of value in 59 percent of the models we ran (Figure 2.4).

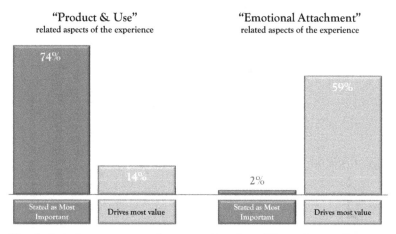

Figure 2.4 *Customers say they want "product," but what really drives business value is "Emotional attachment"*

Sources: When asked to select the most and least important aspects of the experience, 74 percent of the customer groups we analyzed selected a product-related aspect as the most important and only 2 percent selected an emotional aspect as most important.
Yet, *emotional aspects were actually the biggest driver of value* for 59 percent of the customer groups we analyzed.

This shows that customers are not good at articulating what truly matters to them. They are not really aware of the inner drivers of their attitudes and behavior. What I've come to realize with this research is that most of the product-related and functional aspects are just a means to an end for customers, even though they don't realize it. So for example, customers may say that they want a camera or a phone with more pixels but what they really crave is the feeling they'll get when they share and showcase their pictures. So the product (i.e., a phone with a higher resolution camera) is a means to get to an emotional state of pride, joy, fulfillment, and so on when they showcase their pictures.

Here are some more examples from our research:

- Telecom customers in the United States will say that what's most important to them is that the company delivers a reliable network, speed of data services (i.e., Internet), and value for the money plans (all what we would categorize as product-related aspects). However, what drove the most value was the perceived trustworthiness, responsiveness, and empathy of the organization.

- Telecom customers in the UAE and Saudi Arabia were not much different than those in the United States. They said that they wanted the most speed of data services and reliable network and services but what drove the most value was the perceived feeling of a relationship with the organization, the perception that the organization cares for them as a person and that it keeps its promises.

- The customers of one U.S. insurance company would say that what's most important for them is the competitiveness of the rates (product), but what really drove the value metrics was trusting the organization to take care of their claim.

- In the finance sector, the premium charge card customers of one brand said that what's most important to them is the acceptance of the card by merchants, but what really drove value was the feeling of a personalized service, the feeling that the company cares about them and, for the top customers, the feeling of prestige.

- In manufacturing, B2B customers say that the most important to them is dependable products, but what would really make them buy again from them and recommend the manufacturer was the feeling that the organization is responsive, cares for them, respects them, and builds a relationship.

- In IT, B2B customers would say that the most important for them is the ease of using the software (product), but what would make them renew their license and recommend the organization was the feeling that they are being listened to, their concerns are acknowledged, and they are being valued as a customer.

These are just some of the examples from our research and experience over the years where customers say they want a product aspect but it's actually emotional attachment aspects that would "move the needle" for the organization.

One of my favorite examples about the difference between what customers say they want versus what drives value, that is not product related, comes from research with patients and there have been some interesting academic journal articles that are in line with our findings. We asked patients of a U.S. hospital system what is most important for them when interacting with their GP and overwhelmingly the answer was "we want to spend more time with the doctor." This is logical. After all, they take time off work, travel 45 minutes to get to the doctor's office, pay for parking, and insurance co-pay just to spend some time with the doctor, right? However, our analysis showed that what they really wanted was not to spend more mean time with the doctor but to spend quality time. They wanted to feel that the staff cares for them as a person; that they are listened to and their concerns are acknowledged, to feel respected, to feel that their doctor and staff anticipate their needs; and that the doctor "knows" them.

To BATHE or Not to BATHE

As we shared the results of our research with hospital executives, one of them pointed us to a couple of articles published in the *Journal of Family Medicine* that are in line with our findings. The first one, titled "To BATHE or Not to BATHE: Patient Satisfaction With Visits to Their Family Physician" [3] (Family Medicine 2008) looks at how applying the BATHE method increases patient satisfaction in an outpatient setting (i.e., visits to the GP), while the second article, "Effects of a Brief Psychosocial Intervention on Inpatient Satisfaction: A Randomized Controlled Trial" [4] (Family Medicine 2017) looks at applying the method in an inpatient setting (i.e., during a hospital stay).

BATHE is an acronym for Background, Affect, Trouble, Handling, and Empathy and refers to specific questions or comments incorporated into a standard medical interview (Table 2.4). The questions invite "the patient to talk about whatever is important to him or her, and prompts the physician to express empathy and elicit positive coping." [4]

In the outpatient study, patients presenting to a large family practice center in New Brunswick, NJ, would see one of four physicians within the practice.

Table 2.4 BATHE questions

	Example question	Description
Background	"What is going on in your life?"	This question helps elicit the context of the patient's visit
Affect	"How do you feel about that?" or "What is your mood?"	This question allows the patient to report on his/her current feeling state
Trouble	"What about the situation troubles you the most?" or "Is there anything about that that troubles you?"	This question should be asked even when the patient's affect is positive, as they may still be stressed about their current life circumstances
Handling	"How are you handling that?" or "How could you handle that?"	This question is asked to evaluate what psychological stress the patient may be experiencing that may be contributing to their physical complaint or affective state
Empathy	"That must be very difficult for you"	Expressing empathy or sympathy conveys a sense of concern and of being understood, which affirms the patients and enhances positive feelings toward their health care provider

Two physicians were instructed to use the BATHE protocols until data had been collected from 10 patients and then to proceed in their usual fashion with their next 10 patients. The other two physicians conducted their interview as usual with their first 10 patients and then used BATHE with the following 10 patients. All patients were asked to complete a satisfaction survey following their consultation. (This was designed in order to eliminate potential order effects.)

BATHEd patients responded with significantly higher ratings for 8 of the 11 satisfaction measures, including those related to information provided, perception of physician concern, and likelihood of recommending the physician to others. (Leiblum et al. 2008)

The results showed an increase in overall satisfaction with the day's visit by 17.5 percent—patients asked the five BATHE questions returned a mean score of 4.7 versus 4.0 for non-BATHEd patients. Similarly, when asked, "Was your doctor sympathetic to your needs or concerns?" 94.7 percent of the BATHEd respondents responded positively (i.e., with an "yes") versus 75.5 percent of the non-BATHEd respondents. [5]

Other outpatient studies have also found the BATHE intervention to improve patient satisfaction, [6] interestingly, without significantly increasing time spent per office visit. [7, 8]

The BATHE method was proven to increase patient satisfaction in an inpatient setting as well. Subject to the second paper, we mentioned earlier, was a study conducted with 25 patients admitted to the University of Virginia Family Medicine inpatient service. They were randomized to usual care or to the BATHE intervention. Those in the intervention group received the BATHE intervention daily for five days or until discharge. At completion, participants completed a patient satisfaction measure.

Results showed that the "daily administration of BATHE had strong effects on patients' likelihood of endorsing their medical care as 'excellent.'" Overall satisfaction improved by 26 percent (from 3.26 to 4.12 on a 1 to 5 Likert scale). What's interesting is that patients were more satisfied with their hospitalization experience when "physicians take a daily moment to check in with the patient 'as a person' and not just as a medical patient."[9]

The research on the BATHE method is consistent with our findings that listening to patients, acknowledging their concerns, showing that you "know" them by taking an interest in them, and showing that you care for them as a person by expressing empathy increase customer satisfaction. Consequently, it leads to more business value for the organization because, in the United States, patient experience scores are publicly reported on the Centers for Medicare and Medicaid Services Hospital Compare website and are factored into Medicare's value-based payments. [10] Health care organizations focusing on these aspects will also gain value by the increased likelihood of patients to use and recommend the services of the hospital.

This also shows that through intervention, in this case, training on asking five questions to elicit empathy, you can evoke the desired emotions, increase customer satisfaction, and drive business performance.

The examples we provided earlier were mostly about customers saying that what's most important for them was a product aspect whereas, in fact, the biggest driver of value for the organization was an emotional attachment aspect. Of course, this was not the case in all the organizations and customer groups we looked at. In some instances, the biggest drivers of value were "brand"-related attributes such as "a brand I can relate to" or "reliable brand."

The similarity between brand and emotional attachment aspects is that in both cases those are what we would call subconscious drivers. Hardly anyone is stating those as important aspects (how many people have you heard saying "I want more advertising" or "being able to relate to a brand is more important to me than the price"). When we look at the importance scores, we see that "a brand I can relate to" is four to seven times less important to customers than product-related attributes in the respective customer groups. Yet we know that brand perception and advertising drive revenue for businesses, even if customers don't say that they want it. This is a classical case of what we call subconscious drivers.

In the four-box model (Figure 2.5), the horizontal axis looks at what customers say they want (i.e., the desired). The vertical axis looks at what actually drives value for the business (i.e., increase spend, customer

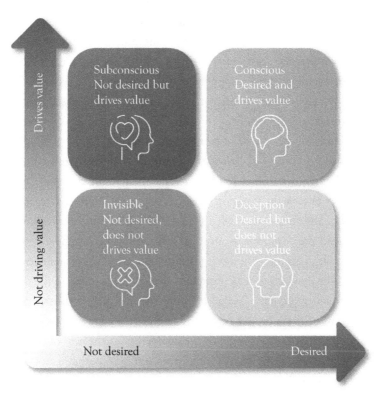

Figure 2.5 Beyond Philosophy's desirability versus value 2×2 box

retention, likelihood to recommend, etc.). Conscious is the category of aspects that are highly desired (customers rank them high in importance to them) and we find that those drive value. On the opposite end of the spectrum is the Invisible category. Those are things that customers don't desire much and don't drive value. If organizations have any feedback mechanism the aspects within these categories shouldn't come as a surprise to them as they'd have either heard customers saying that these things are important to them or never mention them at all. However, the other two categories are typically a surprise. The Subconscious aspects, as the emotional and "brand"-related aspects that we mentioned earlier, are typically not something that will come high up in what customers say they want and brag about but they drive customers' attitudes and behavior. On the other hand, we have the Deception category, where customers say they want something (i.e., more time with the doctor), but this could trick you into spending a lot of time, effort, and money after something, only to see no movement at all in customer satisfaction and operational performance. Think about if you were to go to the CFO and say our research shows that patients want more time with the doctor, you'd have to either see fewer patients per day (less revenue, less availability of appointment slots, longer wait time to get to see your doctor) or employ more doctors (more costs) and then see no increase in patient satisfaction at all! No wonder it took so long for customer experience to take off and still many programs fail to deliver results.

Having said this, it's important to position all of these research findings in the right way. First, you have to take these results as a snapshot in time. They answer the question based on where we are today (regarding product quality, price, etc.), what would make the customer stay with us, recommend us, buy from us more, and so on. So, for example, we did research with customers of a water utility company. Unsurprisingly, the number one thing customers wanted was when they turned on the tap to get clean water (no color, no odor). However, the reality was that that's exactly what they get (99.99 percent of the time). What was actually going to improve their satisfaction with the company was the ease of problem resolution, the resolving of recurring issues, and so on. That is not to say that the company needs to stop investing in the cleanliness of the water.

If the water coming out of the tap was to turn yellow, we'd likely get different results. What it meant was that in order to improve customer satisfaction they had to focus not so much on the #1 thing customers said they want (clean water) but on the #1 driver of customer satisfaction—in this case, ease of problem resolution. Similarly, we did research with a container shipping company in the midst of the downturn from the financial crisis in 2008. We found the drivers of value in their experience, and at the time, having analyzed 15 customer segments, the availability of shipping equipment didn't come up at all. We repeated the research the next year when shipping had picked up again, and this time the availability of shipping equipment was a big driver in all models. The market had changed! Therefore, when we say this or that product aspect doesn't drive value, it doesn't mean to drop it altogether, to raise the prices, and so on. It means that for that particular customer group, at that moment in time, there are other things that the organization can do to drive profitable customer behavior.

The second thing is that often different aspects might be more or less important depending on where in the sales funnel customers are. For example, the price aspect might be a key driving point for customers looking to choose their energy provider, but once they are in, it could be that some experience aspects become the key driving factor for their decision whether to renew their contract or not. Typically, in our experience, we've seen that when the prices are more or less on par with the competition, then there are other things that play a bigger role when customers choose one company over another. So, in the example with energy customers, when we had done research with them we had found that when the price is on par with the competition, customers were looking at the customer satisfaction star rating, customer comments on how easy it is to speak to a representative, and the brand was what we'd call a subconscious driver. When you see an offer, even if it's slightly cheaper but from a company you never heard of and on the other side there is a brand you know of, customers were more likely to go with the company they knew (comparing price, customer satisfaction ratings, and brand perception). We mentioned that people prefer to go with brands they know of—this could be related to a behavioral science principle called the "mere-exposure effect," which basically states that people tend to develop a preference for people and things as a consequence of repeated exposure to them.

Then, we talk about price; a typical behavioral science principle in play is extremeness aversion. This is the tendency of choice makers to avoid extreme options and choose an intermediate option. This way, whether you are choosing a bottle of wine or a washing machine, typically, people don't choose the most expensive nor the cheapest (this must have to do with their self-esteem and self-perceived image), but go for a middle option. However, that is not always the case. When we were talking about behavioral science and emotions to a premium tire manufacturer, representatives from a wealthy Middle-East country came to us during the break and told us a story. They had a problem with sales and on talking to customers they realized that customers saw the price as an indication of product quality and luxury and they wanted to buy the best (i.e., what they really wanted was the feeling of self-esteem and prestige from buying the most expensive brand). So contrary to the conventional economic theory about the price-elasticity of demand, they actually got more sales when they increased the price. This is an example of how irrational customer behavior actually is and how emotional drivers and price are intertwined.

Emotions Have a Big Impact on Business Value

So far, the biggest takeaways from our research were that emotional attachment drives the most business value and that customers don't really know what they want the most. The third big takeaway from our research is that emotions affect about 50 percent of business value. Now, how is this different from the first finding? Remember the "stimulus–response–effect" model we discussed earlier? We treated the aspects that we grouped under "Emotional attachment" the same way we treated the rest of the touchpoints of the experience (e.g., customer service, digital self-service channels, product). This was so we could compare all these touchpoints as "apples to apples" and see which has the most effect on business value. Under "Emotional attachment" we had aspects that differ from our 20 emotions-set (Figure 1.1) such as "feel like I have a relationship with the company," "respects me," "cares for me as a person," "cares about my success," "treats me as a valued business partner," and "feel appreciated." In the model, we linked all the touchpoints to the positive and negative emotions and also to the value indicators (likelihood to recommend, likelihood to renew, etc.) and tested the links for statistical significance and root-cause analysis. This way, each touchpoint could have a direct effect on the business value indicator, an indirect effect (drives/destroys particular emotions and in turn, those emotions drive or destroy business value), or both.

When we looked and summed up the direct and indirect effects of the touchpoints on business value we discovered that emotions affect 48 percent of business value (48 percent in B2B and 49 percent in B2C; Table 2.5).

Table 2.5 Emotion's effect on value: B2B versus B2C results

	B2B	B2C
Direct effects	52%	51%
Negative emotions	24%	20%
Positive emotions	24%	29%

This is huge! Why? Because most organizations don't do research on emotions or don't include emotions as part of their analysis. This means (1) the results and conclusions they reach do not reflect the true world and (2) they miss the cause for about 50 percent of business value (customer attitudes toward the brand). By not including emotions in their research, organizations fail to notice the impact that they have, they fail to notice the impact that subconscious aspects in the experience have on emotions, and thus they fail to act on aspects of the experience that will actually generate the most business value for the organization. The range of what they focus on and act on is limited by what they fail to notice.

Now let's do a quick recap of our research. We found that:

- Emotional attachment aspects are by far the biggest driver of value for organizations, followed by the aspects falling in the "Product" category (i.e., price, quality, etc.) and the "Brand & advertising" category.

- o When we say "value" for organizations we mean proxies for future financial performance such as likelihood for customers to buy again from them, recommend them to a friend, preference for the organization over their competitors, and ease of doing business with an organization.
- Customers, however, are not aware of what really drives their attitude toward organizations. They say that the most important for them are product-related aspects and yet it is emotional attachment aspects that drive their attitude in most cases. This shows that emotional aspects affect the customer behavior oftentimes on an unconscious level.
- Emotions affect about 50 percent of business value.

Together these findings, that is, that emotional attachment is the biggest driver of value and that customers are oftentimes unaware or not able to articulate the true drivers of their attitudes and behavior toward brands, are fundamental. Why? Because they mean that most organizations miss on the biggest driver of customer behavior and consequently business value. And by not measuring emotions they miss about 50 percent of the picture and thus are not able to register how important emotions are compared to other aspects of the experience. But don't just take our word for it...

Before we discuss what these results mean for organizations and what they should do in Part II of the book, we'll provide some more evidence from other researchers about the effect of emotional attachment on business value (Chapter 3) and explain these results through the prism of psychology (Chapter 4).

CHAPTER 3

Evidence From Independent Research

Our relationships are stronger when we perceive that our partners are responsive to us.

—Professor Harry T. Reis

Similar to how when you are looking to buy a car in a given color (say a green Subaru) and suddenly you start to see these cars all over the place (a hint, their numbers haven't increased magically overnight, just you notice them more), after I completed the analysis of our database and especially after I started thinking about writing this book, I started to come across other pieces of research that align with my findings. Behavioral science may call this "Baader-Meinhof phenomenon". It's named after a militant West German terrorist group, active in the 1970s. It was, however, in 1994 (decades after the group was disbanded) when a press commenter dubbed the frequency illusion "the Baader-Meinhof phenomenon" after randomly hearing two references to Baader-Meinhof within 24 hours. [1] So I may be biased after all but the research I'll share with you here has a sound scientific base.

The Science of Personal Relationships

What makes some relationships endure while others fail?

Harry Reis, a professor of psychology at the University of Rochester, has spent a lifetime studying the science of personal relationships, following the work of others in the field, and conducting hundreds of experiments. Before we give you his conclusion as to what makes or breaks our relationships with loved ones, here is another, supposedly easier question:

What makes the behavior of two partners in a close relationship different from the behavior of two independent individuals?

Summarizing the literature review on the subject, Reis concludes that it comes down to the ability to influence each other's emotions and moods the way others can't. And when we say influence each other's emotions, we mean not just evoke emotions but also affect the ability to self-regulate our emotions (i.e., when feeling down, stressed, or pissed off and we feel the support of the partner we can manage and regulate those negative feelings more easily). Because when we feel that our partner is responding supportively toward our important needs, goals, values, or preferences, then our "emotional well-being is enhanced and effective emotional self-regulation is facilitated." [2] When the opposite happens, and we don't feel understood and supported by our partners, our emotional well-being suffers, and emotional self-regulation is impaired. In other words, "our emotional lives are intrinsically and often profoundly influenced by the behavior of close others" and when we try to regulate these emotions, we often "anticipate and perceive our partner's response to our expression of emotion." Reis refers to this phenomenon as "perceived partner responsiveness."

Here are some examples of how partners influence each other's emotions ("affective interdependence," as academics call it). You know how you start an argument with your partner over a small thing, and then you both get angry. Just as I am writing these lines, our 2-year-old pissed in his pants, and we started arguing whose fault it is and who has to go and change him now. But at the same time, when we see him joyful, when we see him riding his bike, or playing with other children it makes us happy too. Similarly, elderly couples look at pictures of past experiences they have shared and cherish the memories. At the same time, each partner could get annoyed and disappointed over the lack of interest or support from their partner on issues they are concerned with. So partners have the ability to influence each other's emotions, support each other, and share the good and bad times the way others can't.

Going back to the original question, why do some relationships endure while others fall apart? Reis presents his candidate for the "central organizing principle" of relationship science—a concept that could tie together the vast and scattered research literature. It can be captured in one sentence: Our relationships are stronger when we *perceive* that our *partners* are *responsive* to us [3] (or "perceived partner responsiveness" as is often referred to in academic literature).

Responsiveness encompasses three things:

1. *Understanding*: My partner knows me and what is important to me.
2. *Validation*: My partner values and appreciates my abilities, traits, and worldview (i.e., the emotion of feeling respected).
3. *Caring*: My partner takes active and supportive steps in helping me meet my needs (i.e. the emotion of feeling cared for).

Now see these statements as if they come from a customer!

According to Reis, *understanding* matters and is the starting point because it fosters a sense of authenticity and drives the next two factors. *Validation* matters because making the partner feel respected and valued supports the feeling of belonging and security. Finally, *caring* demonstrates the concern for one's well-being.

The work of Harry T. Reis rang home with me as I was looking at the results of the research. He mentions things like "responsiveness," "understanding," "respect," "caring." When we look into the aspects that form the "Emotional attachment" (Table 2.3), we see the same things, for example, feeling cared for, feeling the organization is responsive, feeling respect, and feeling listened to (a necessary prelude to "understanding"). Therefore, what makes personal relationships endure is also what makes business relationships endure and what makes customers form an emotional attachment toward brands!

Emotional Brand Attachment

Research from other organizations also confirms the importance of emotional attachment. Motista collected data from 2016 to 2018 from more than 100,000 customers of more than 100 retailers across multiple sectors. They found that customers who feel an emotional connection to a brand are far more valuable to retailers, in some cases spending twice as much, than customers who rate themselves as satisfied with the brand (CSAT). Additionally, these emotionally connected customers have a 306 percent higher lifetime value (LTV), stay with a brand for an average of 5.1 years versus 3.4 years, and will recommend brands at a much higher rate (71 percent vs. 45 percent). [4]

This is remarkable because it's based on actual behavior and spend data and it shows that the emotional connection is a better predictor of customer's behavior, LTV, and growth potential than metrics like customer satisfaction.

Now, how do they define emotional connection? In the study report, they say "An emotional connection occurs when people connect their values, desires, or aspirations to a brand. These connections often live in the unconscious and go unspoken." [5] The second part of their definition goes back to what we were saying earlier about the "subconscious" aspects of the experience and the examples we provided about the difference between what customers (and patients) say they want and what actually drives their behavior (and business value).

Let's go back to the first part of the definition. In the study report, they don't give more concrete examples of how they've measured the emotional connection but they provide such examples in previous reports. In the *Harvard Business Review* (HBR) paper "The New Science of Customer Emotions" (2015), Motista authors Scott Magids, Alan Zorfas, and Daniel Leemon provide pretty much the same definition as stated earlier and follow up: "Important emotional motivators include desires to 'stand out from the crowd,' 'have confidence in the future,' and 'enjoy a sense of well-being,' to name just a few." [6] In another Motista report, "Ranking Emotional Connection: A Look at 50 of the Top U.S. Brands" they add examples such as "a sense of belonging, the brand makes them feel like they'll succeed in life, a sense of security, they feel admired, or they feel a sense of thrill." [7]

Although they are more centered around the brand connection and more marketing oriented, their findings align with ours and some of their "emotional motivators" are similar to what we had in some of our studies. They too argue in the HBR article that although companies know in general that emotions drive customer behavior, what they do is mostly guesswork, rather than a rigorous systematic approach based on science and data that looks to identify the right emotions to target at the right moments of the customer journey (i.e., the emotions that attract prospects to become customers may be different than those that would drive retention or would make them use more products and services). In other words, emotions "in general" don't drive value, but specific emotions do and companies need to find the specific emotional drivers in their customer journey.

Another organization, MBLM, which uses a distinctive index to measure the customer's intimacy with an organization also found that brands that nurture emotional bonds with their customers tend to outperform top companies listed on the S&P 500 and Fortune 500 in both revenue and profit. [8] Not only that, but they can also build higher levels of trust, which in turn breeds a more loyal consumer base over time. MBLM reports in their Brand Intimacy Covid Study [9] that "Intimate brands" posted revenue growth for Q2 2020 versus Q2 2019 that was 1.44 percent higher compared to S&P 500 and 4.28 percent higher than Fortune 500. Their stock price outperformed S&P 500 by 3.67 percent and the Fortune 500 by 24.1 percent. Profit growth for the same period outperformed the two indexes by a staggering 101.1 percent and 76.48 percent, respectively.

The way MBLM determines an emotional connection is "by the degree of overall positive feelings a customer has toward a brand and the extent to which a person associates the brand with key attributes." [10] The attributes are around (1) fulfillment, that is, whether or not the brand delivers superior quality and service; (2) identity, that is, whether the brand reflects an aspirational image (think of American Express Centurion Card) and admired values (think of clothing retailer Patagonia and cosmetics retailer Lush); (3) enhancement, that is, becoming better through use of the brand (think of Apple laptops and smartphones); (4) ritual, that is, the habitual use of the brand and it being ingrained in your daily routine (think of Starbucks, your phone, car, etc.); (5) nostalgia, that is, focuses on memories of the past (think of Disney, Campbell's soup, etc.); and (6) indulgent, that is, creates a close relationship centered around moments of pampering and gratification (think expensive chocolates, Ben & Jerry's, Starbucks, etc.).

Some further evidence comes from customer experience research firm Forrester who found that the way customers *feel* about a brand (i.e., variables that describe traditional brand characteristics—"helpful," "trustworthy," etc.), as well as emotions they may feel during a brand experience ("disgust," "delight," etc.), has 1.5 times more impact on business outcomes than how they *think* about it (i.e., variables that describe attributes or actions a brand may take in general, like "provides great recommendations," "fits my lifestyle," and "has friendly employees"). [11]

There is a lot of evidence at a company level as well. In the B2B hardware and software sector, a company shared with us that they had found that the more advanced feeling of a relationship (i.e., perceiving the vendor as a trusted advisor as opposed to just a vendor) meant a 45 percent increase in actual spend with them. Similarly, a global logistics company reported to us that they had found that emotions were the primary driver of brand attachment. This meant real financial benefits to them as they had also found that the more attached customers are the higher their share of shipment with the organization is. "Attached" customers were also more likely to use a wider variety of products thus yielding higher revenues. The way they had defined brand attachment included a combination of attributes including customer willingness to drive further just to get to their office, willingness to pay premium prices, and so on.

The evidence shared in this chapter that emotional attachment is key for business outcomes is eye-opening:

- What makes our personal relationships with our partners endure are the same things that create the feeling of a relationship and an emotional attachment in customers toward organizations. The work of professor Harry T. Reis shows that what makes or breaks personal relationships is whether we feel our partners are *responsive* to us, whether we feel they "know us" and understand us, that they *appreciate* us, *respect* us, make us feel *valued* and *cared for*, they are supportive of our needs, and we can *trust* them. Now read these as if they relate to the B2C relationship because all those were aspects that our research found to be key drivers of business value.

- Research firm Motista, having analyzed data of the behavior of more than 100,000 customers of more than 100 retailers across multiple sectors, found that customers who feel an emotional connection to a brand are far more valuable to retailers than customers who rate themselves as satisfied with the brand (CSAT). They spend a lot more and stay for longer and will recommend the brand at a much higher rate.
- Another organization, MBLM, also found that brands that nurture emotional bonds with their customers tend to outperform top companies listed on the S&P 500 and Fortune 500 in both revenue and profit.

There are of course many other studies and we'll share some more later on that relate more to emotions in marketing. For now, I'll stop here at this point as given the overwhelming evidence that emotions have the potential to drive a great deal of value to businesses and yet customers themselves may not be aware of their inner desires and drivers, an interesting question is why is this the case. We will try to answer that in the next chapter.

CHAPTER 4

The Psychological Explanation

We actually don't choose between experiences, we choose between memories of experiences.

—Professor Daniel Kahneman

In the previous two chapters, we provided astounding evidence both from our research and from independent research that emotions are key drivers of value for organizations. But why are they so important and yet, customers themselves are not aware of their importance to them? We'll dig into this question in this chapter.

Why Are Emotions So Important?

Behavioral science comes to the forefront in explaining why emotions are so important. Professor Daniel Kahneman, Nobel Laureate for economics, says, "There is confusion between experience and memories. We actually don't choose between experiences, we choose between memories of experiences." [1] He, therefore, distinguishes between two "self"-s, the "experiencing self" which is us while being on a vacation, attending a concert, or having an experience with an organization, and the "remembering self," which is us a few days, weeks, months after having had those experiences.

One of the experiments that professor Kahneman conducted involved patients undergoing a colonoscopy procedure, which at the time was quite an unpleasant and painful procedure. Two groups of participants were asked to keep a record of the level of pain they had experienced throughout the procedure. The difference was that with group B, at the end, they left the tube for the procedure for slightly longer in the patient's body without moving it too much so there is a moment of reduced pain just before they take it out. That made the "experiencing self" worse off because every minute of the unpleasant experience that the "remembering self" had, it had too and even more, but it turned out that the "remembering self" was better off as patients in group B rated the experience as not nearly as bad as patients in group A, who had a shorter experience but whose experience ended in a high level of pain.

This and other experiments led Kahneman and his fellow researchers to suggest that people judge an experience not based on the sum of all the moments but based on how they felt at the peak of the experience and at the end. This is known as the peak–end rule and in our opinion is one of the most profound principles of behavioral science.

What this means is that what matters more are the memories customers take from the experiences they have with organizations, because when the time comes for them to renew their subscription or buy again from an organization, it won't be their "experiencing self" that makes the decision but rather their "remembering self," that is, their memories from the experience they had with an organization.

And what creates memories? We know that the greater an emotion is felt, the more vivid is the recollection of that experience. We may forget the transactional side of the experience but it is the emotional peak and ending moments that stick with us. Think about the time your favorite basketball team won the NBA or the time your child had a severe illness. You'll most likely remember where you were on September 11, 2001, and what that day looked like but you'd hardly recall what you did the previous day. Similarly, you may vividly recall your first kiss with your loved one but don't remember what you did together last Tuesday. These moments stand in your memory unlike many others because those were moments of intense emotions.

In the book *Memory and Emotion* (Oxford University Press 2004), editors Daniel Reisberg and Paula Hertel review in depth the numerous academic research on the link between emotions and memory. They say that "Emotion's capacity to promote memory for an event's gist or center has been demonstrated in many settings, both inside the laboratory and out." [2] They provide examples of many experiments which look at the various aspects of memory and emotional stimuli. Experiments described in the book range from relying on participants to self-rate their emotionality to an event and then self-rate whether they believed they could remember the event, to being shown slides and videos of both emotionally charged and neutral content, to real-life events and so on. They all show a linkage between stronger emotion and memory recall. Among the many interesting examples was a study by Bluck and Li (2001) which showed that the strength of participants' emotional feelings about the O.J. Simpson's verdict was predictive of how fully the event was recalled eight months later.

It is therefore important to understand that one of the reasons why emotions are so important in business is that people don't choose between experiences; they choose between the memories of their experiences and the stronger the emotions customers felt (good or bad), the stronger their memory of that experience will be. Treat the prior statement as a general rule of thumb as to every rule there are exceptions of course (those who have studied French would know this very well). In some cases, the extreme feeling of fear and stress may lead our brain to crash and lose the memory of that event altogether but I won't go into too much detail on this topic.

The peak–end rule really is a fundamental principle and we'll discuss how we have applied it in the design of an experience in Chapter 5, and in Chapter 13 we'll show further evidence, coming from an AI-trained algorithm on millions of customer interactions with call center agents, that shows again just how powerful this principle actually is.

In the previous chapters, we have provided overwhelming evidence both from our research and from that of others that emotions drive a great deal of value in business. In Figure 2.4 we showed that in our research emotional attachment was the biggest driver of value for 59 percent of the customer groups and yet just 2 percent of the groups did state an emotional attachment aspect as most important. What did the rest state is most important to them? In 70 percent of the groups, customers said that the most important to them is a product-related aspect (i.e., price, reliability, etc.). This shows the discrepancy between what customers say they want from organizations and what actually drives their attitudes and behavior toward those organizations. We have shown that one of the reasons emotions might play such an important role is that those are intrinsically linked to customers' memories of events and interactions and when the time comes for customers to choose who to buy from, those memories come to the forefront. But why is it that customers are not able to articulate what is truly important to them (i.e., what drives their behavior)? We'll now look into this.

Why Can't Customers Articulate the Real Drivers of Their Behavior?

Studies on brain-split patients have marked the career of Dr. Michael Gazzaniga, the director of the Center for Cognitive Neuroscience at Dartmouth. He began his career in the lab of Dr. Roger W. Sperry, a California Institute of Technology neuroscientist who won the 1981 Nobel Prize in medicine for his studies on the connection between the brain's hemispheres. Our brains have two hemispheres, with the right one being linked to the left side of our body and vice versa. The two hemispheres communicate through a bundle of fibers called corpus callosum. Surgeons sometimes cut the corpus callosum of people with severe epilepsy to reduce their seizures. Dr. Gazzaniga spent time studying such patients. One such patient was W.J. who could put together a puzzle with his left or right hand but not with the two hands at the same time. This showed that the human brain hemispheres became isolated as well and operated independently of one another.

Later, Dr. Gazzaniga and Dr. Joseph LeDoux, now at New York University, conducted an experiment with a patient called P.S. as reported in the *New York Times* article by Carl Zimmer "Scientist at Work: Michael Gazzaniga; A Career Spent Learning How the Mind Emerges From the Brain" [3] (2005). They showed P.S. a picture and asked him to choose a related image from a set of other pictures. The patient did not know that he was actually shown different images to the left and the right eyes. What happened next was crucial for our understanding of how the mind works.

P.S. was shown a picture of a chicken claw in his right eye and a snow-covered house in the left eye, so when it came to selecting relevant pictures, he pointed to a chicken with his right hand and a snow shovel with his left. When they asked him "Why did you do that?" P.S. says "The chicken claw goes with the chicken." So far so good, as this is what the left hemisphere of the brain saw (remember the right side of the body is linked to the left hemisphere). Then P.S. looks at the shovel and says, "The reason you need a shovel is to clean out the chicken shed."

This is the interesting part: P.S.'s left hemisphere of the brain made up a story to explain his actions based on the limited information it had. With his left eye, associated with the right hemisphere of the brain, P.S. had seen the snow-covered house and thus unconsciously made the association with the snow shovel, but the left hemisphere had not seen the snow-covered house so made up the story about needing the shovel to clean the chicken shed. Since then Dr. Gazzaniga has carried out hundreds of similar experiments with his colleagues and the left hemisphere has consistently acted this way. So he and his colleagues in the 1970s called the left hemisphere "The Interpreter" because, acting as an interpreter, it was creating theories to make sense of a person's experiences. In other words, some of our actions might be driven by something that originated in our right brain hemisphere but are then explained by the left brain hemisphere, which comes up with some logical explanation of our actions… Sounds familiar?

Let me give you some examples. Once I decided to trade my three-series BMW for a five-series one, bigger and twice more powerful than the old one. I rationalized the purchase to my fiancée, who was saying "why spend the money, we are fine with this car," by answering that I'm driving longer distances and need more boot space. The reality was that my friends had both Audis with 3.0-liter engines and said to me, "one day you'll drive one of these and you'll see what it is." I'm sure similar things have happened to you, whether you were buying a car, an expensive watch, a smartphone, or a camera. As a matter of fact, I remember one of my senior consultant colleagues who was joking that every time he is considering buying a piece of electronics he makes a list of the key attributes that matter the most to him, compares the different brands, and every time he ends up buying Sony. Colin Shaw, my mentor, a fan of Apple, knows that he'll do the same at the end and doesn't even bother doing lists and just buys Apple.

There is even evidence for this at a large scale too. Growing up in the Balkans and then living in the United Kingdom I couldn't help but read an article that called "The Bankan Syndrome" the fact that the region had the highest per capita rate of 4x4 cars while the United Kingdom had the highest per capita rate of convertibles. Just for a reference, back in the days when I was young and had a manual A/C in the car, in early August, I'd drive north across Europe to go back to the United Kingdom from summer vacation. When I got home to the UK I'd turn off the A/C ...and I wouldn't turn it back on until next May–June time. So convertibles in the United Kingdom are not the most practical cars either but they had the highest per capita rate of them in Europe.

So what does this all mean? It means that much of our behavior occurs without conscious thought or is based on emotions and impulses that aren't processed in the cognitive areas of our brains. Harvard Business School professor Gerald Zaltman says that "95 percent of our purchase decision making takes place in the subconscious mind." [4] The subconscious is the process and thought of which we are not aware, the "human operating system." We are not aware of it running but the subconscious has a surprising effect on what we do.

Yet, we are hardly ever short on answers. We rationalize postpurchase and come up with logical explanations for our behavior. Let me share with you one of my favorite experiments. Researchers Adrian North and his colleagues Hargreaves and McKendrick from the University of Leicester, United Kingdom, played traditional French and German music in a supermarket. [5] The French and German wines were matched for price and flavor. Consistent with this priming, on French music days, 77 percent of the wine sold was French, on German music days 73 percent was German. Music primed certain thoughts and people reacted accordingly.

The interesting part is that only 1 out of 44 customers who agreed to answer some questions at the checkout spontaneously mentioned the music as the reason they bought the wine. People said they bought the wine because "it was the right price," "I liked the label," and so on. When asked specifically, if they thought that the music affected their choice 86 percent said that it didn't. The behavioral influence of the music was massive, but the customers didn't notice or believe that it was affecting them.

Remember the statistics and examples we shared earlier about customers saying that product aspects are the most important for them and yet it is emotional and subconscious aspects that drive their behavior. Here's why they don't know what really drives them. They are driven by emotion or an unconscious desire but when asked their "Interpreter" brain makes a story and comes up with the most logical explanation.

This helps explain why certain things don't show on an organization's radars. Traditional research is not well equipped to uncover subconscious stimuli and emotional impulses. To avoid missing out on those key drivers of customer behavior, organizations need to rely less on what customers say rationally and consciously that they want and dive deeper into their unconscious drivers, emotional motivators, implicit behavior, and more into the customers' irrationality, which we'll talk about as follows.

How We Think: Two Systems

Now, think about the times you've been "of two minds" about something, whether it was about having a cake for dessert when you said to yourself that you'll go on a diet or your gut was telling you not to trust that sales agent but the offer seemed of really good value? In all these cases our two minds are in conflict.

People have been talking about the two minds influencing their thoughts and behavior since at least the days of Aristotle. Most commonly, people talk about the heart and mind. In recent psychology and behavioral science literature, the standard protocol for naming the two distinctive ways our brain has for thinking about things is System 1 and System 2. This is also the labeling adopted by Nobel Prize laureate psychologist Daniel Kahneman in his book *Thinking Fast and Slow* (2011). System 1 is more intuitive and automatic while System 2 is more reflective and rational. As System 1 and System 2 are not so descriptive names that make it easy for nonpsychologists to recall which one was which, professor Richard Thaler, another behavioral scientist laureate of the Nobel Prize, in his book *Nudge: Improving Decisions About Health, Wealth, and Happiness*, calls them the Automatic System and the Reflective System. My friends and colleagues Colin Shaw and professor Ryan Hamilton chose to call them the Intuitive System and the Rational System in their book *The Intuitive Customer: 7 Imperatives for Moving Your Customer Experience to the Next Level* (Palgrave Macmillan 2016). (I'd highly recommend all three books mentioned in this paragraph.)

The Intuitive System is the one we use when we make quick, instant decisions and when we say my "gut/intuition tells me." It is switched "on" all the time but the mental process is automatic and not under your conscious control. We do not have to "think" to make a decision, come up with an answer, or do something. The Intuitive System can be taught. Think about how you learned to type on a computer keyboard or drive. It took some time and lots of repetition but now it's instinctive and you type superfast without even looking at the keys (most of the time anyway). However, I'm sure that if I ask you to recreate the keyboard on a blank piece of paper your conscious mind will struggle (there have actually been such tests among professional typewriters). The same is true about driving. You had to learn about keeping the car within the lanes, working with the pedals, shifting gears for those of us old enough to have driven manual cars, driving in reverse, parking, and so on. Now you don't even need to think about these things. You do them all "on autopilot" (don't mean the Tesla one) while thinking about work and everything else but driving.

Because the Intuitive System is fast, while thinking slows you down, in sports, many coaches are trying to get their teams and players to play a more intuitive and fast game through lots of exercises and repetition. This is implemented in football, basketball, soccer, and even in golf (where people are told "trust your instincts, don't think too much").

The Intuitive System is also the one responsible for recognizing emotions. Have a look at this picture.

Photo by Matheus Ferrero on Unsplash

I'm sure that as soon as you saw the picture, you could recognize what the people in it are likely to feel. You did not have to "think" about it. Now look at the following math problem:

$$237 \times 53$$

Those of you who like challenges (and math) may take a stab at it, while others will simply save themselves the effort and cognitive depletion. Therein lies the main difference between the two systems. The Rational System is more deliberate and conscious; we use it to make complex calculations and decisions, to learn new things but using it for longer periods of time is exhaustive. In such situations, when we are cognitively depleted we are less likely to resist temptations coming from our Intuitive System. By the way, the answer to the above math problem is 12,561.

One of my favorite experiments that illustrate this was shared with me by professor Ryan Hamilton. Researchers asked a group of participants to memorize one of two numbers, telling them they'll have to recite it later. Half the group had to memorize a two-digit number (a relatively easy task, requiring little cognitive effort), while the other half had to try and recall a seven-digit number (a more difficult task, requiring more cognitive resources). Then participants were offered the choice of two desserts: a healthy fruit salad option and a very tempting chocolate cake that doesn't gel well with diets. Guess what! Simply giving people a longer number to remember significantly increased the preference for the cake: 63 percent of the participants in the seven-digit group chose the cake versus 41 percent in the two-digit group. [6] That is because your Rational System has less energy to fight the impulses coming from your Intuitive System. No wonder you feel you deserve a drink after a hard day in the office or a treat on Friday evening. This is a simple example of how the Rational and the Intuitive Systems interact. The Rational System can *approve* the urges of the Intuitive System justifying that you indeed deserve a treat after a hard-working day or *neglect* to override the urges of the Intuitive System as in the experiment with the fruit salad and the cake. *Override* is another way the two systems interact. That happens when the Rational System *overrides* our intuitive response to things and replaces it with a response of its own. A fourth way the two systems interact is when the Intuitive System influences the Rational System. That happens when the Rational System rejects a suggestion from the Intuitive System but

the seed is already planted and makes the Rational System more susceptible to approve the suggestion next time.

This shows the many ways the Intuitive System influences our decision making and behavior. One might be tempted to think that we
should be striving to exercise more self-control and override the decisions coming from the Intuitive System. After all, the Intuitive System
is emotional, perceptual, and automatic. However, this may not always
lead to better decisions. In a series of experiments Ap Dijksterhuis, professor at Radboud University Nijmegen, named among the top 100 most
influential Dutch people, along with colleagues, shows how in many
instances unconscious thought, as he describes it, can lead to better decisions. What's unconscious thought process? You know how they tell you
to postpone a decision and "sleep on it first." Ap along with colleagues
decided to test the scientific merits of this "folk belief."

In one experiment, they asked participants to choose between four
hypothetical apartments. The experiment was such that one of the four
apartments was objectively more desirable than the other but it wasn't
immediately obvious as the apartments were described with a great deal
of information. Some of the participants had to make their decision
immediately after reading all the information while the others did so after
a period of distraction during which they did other things. The researcher's
hypothesis was that the group would continue to "unconsciously think"
about the apartments. The results showed that indeed the "unconscious
thinkers" did better with 60 percent of them choosing the right apartment
versus just 37 percent of the immediate decision makers. Their finding
that unconscious thinkers outperform conscious thinkers and immediate
decision makers has been replicated in a number of other experiments
and interesting domains including clinical diagnoses made by clinical
psychology students and judgments of justice in hypothetical court cases. [7]
Ap gives two reasons why unconscious thought is so helpful. The first
relates to the processing power of conscious and unconscious thought.
"Consciousness works in a serial fashion and has a small capacity," he
says. That is, it can only do one thing at a time, and it can only work on
a very limited amount of information. Unconscious processes have the
capacity to work on different things in parallel and can integrate a large
amount of information. The second reason the unconscious thought is

helpful is that it seems to be better at weighting the relative importance of different attributes. It seems that when we sleep on things or during unconscious thought we can distinguish better the more important from less important aspects.

So how does all this relate to customer experience? Customers often have to make decisions that are based on a great deal of complex information. They take into account their existing experience with the organization, all the times they interacted with that organization (at least those that stuck in their memory), all the advertising and things they've seen in the media. In many instances, they also weigh in their product offering, the price, and so on versus that of competitors. That is a lot to take into account and there may be a lot of unconscious thought that goes on where many aspects would be influencing our "gut feel." As we've quoted professor Gerald Zaltman earlier, 95 percent of our purchase decision making happens in the subconscious mind. Our Intuitive System influences the Rational System and sends impulses to it, which the latter can approve, neglect to take corrective action, or override. Customers may thus be unaware of the things that have the biggest influence on their attitudes and behavior toward organizations.

Going back to that example about the music influencing wine purchase decisions, our Rational System doesn't even know what is going on beneath the surface where our Intuitive System is bringing memories and making associations between French music and images we aspire to. Without knowing it, these subtle clues make us feel a sudden desire for French wine. When asked about it later, our rational brain (the interpreter as Dr. Gazzaniga calls it) refuses to attribute the wine decision to the music and comes up with a story about why we did what we did.

All these psychological findings have implications for businesses. The fact that people are often unaware of the real drivers of their behavior and when asked can't really articulate them but instead make up stories should be taken into account when businesses do research with customers. We'll discuss this in more detail in Part II of the book. The fact that sometimes people use the Rational System to make a decision and sometimes the Intuitive System is interesting on its own. We'll touch on it mostly in light of marketing campaigns for two reasons. One is that the focus in this book is mostly about how to create an emotional connection with customers.

The second reason is that Colin and Ryan have already looked at the implications for customer experience of this and many other behavioral science principles in their aforementioned book *The Intuitive Customer*. One short piece of advice I'd give to organizations is to think through which systems their customers will use when making a decision and to equip their agents with the tools to appeal to both systems (depending on who they are talking to). Facts, specs, comparisons, academic literature, and so on will appeal to the Rational System, while stories, anecdotes, catchy descriptions, and more emotion-targeted content will appeal to the Intuitive System. In some instances, during the sales cycle, customers will move from using mostly their Rational System to a place where the decision feels more intuitive and that should be the objective for all interactions. The decision should feel more intuitive and easy to make.

Let's recap the fascinating research shared in this chapter and what it means:

- Professor Danie Kahneman, Nobel Laureate for economics, says that it is the memories of the experience that really matter because "people don't choose between experiences, they choose between the memories of their experiences." And what do people remember from an experience? Kahneman says that people judge an experience by how they felt at its peak (positive or negative) and at the end. This is known as the "peak–end rule."
- Numerous studies on the link between memory and emotions suggest that stronger emotions (again positive or negative) are associated with stronger memories.
- This could explain why emotions play such an important role when it comes to choosing to buy again from an organization, renew a contract or a subscription, recommend the organization, and so on.
- However, most of the time people might be unaware of what really influences them (e.g., music in the wine store, emotional urges, unconscious references to memories from the past), and when asked what is important to them they use their Rational System (System 2) and it is their "Interpreter

Brain" (as Dr. Gazzaniga calls it) that comes up with a story and an explanation.

- It is therefore important for businesses not just to rely solely on the rational answers that customers give and what they say is important to them, but to dig deeper to find those emotional or unconscious motivators for the customer behavior and do more implicit research.

Let's clarify a couple of things. The aforementioned is an explanation why sometimes customers are not really aware of what drives their behavior and they say that they want one thing (e.g., the card to be more accepted) but it's something else that drives their behavior (e.g., feeling of prestige). That is not to say that we make all decisions using our Intuitive System (System 1). As we've said, sometimes the Rational System (System 2) can override decisions by the Intuitive System. So, for example, the Rational System can say, "No, we won't eat the cake, we want to be healthy and in good sports condition as we have a football game on Sunday." What we know from the research of Antonio Damasio is that emotions are intrinsically linked to decision making. So in the example above, emotions might be influencing your System 1 thinking by craving an instant reward and the feeling of pleasure eating the cake while on the other side, the Rational System (System 2) might be overriding the urges of the Intuitive System while it itself is being influenced by craving the feeling of fulfillment, pride, and joy from being in good shape or winning the football game on Sunday. The human brain is so complex, isn't it!

So far we've shared overwhelming research about the role and importance of emotions and how often people are driven by unconscious aspects and desires that they are unable to articulate (but nevertheless will come up with an explanation). We've also tried to shed some light on how our mind works and explain some of the underlying reasons for the aforementioned findings. In the next part of the book we'll talk about what this all means for organizations and, if emotions are such a big driver of customer attitudes and behavior, how can organizations approach creating an emotional attachment as a science and a strategy.

PART II

What Organizations Need to Do Tomorrow— The Seven Business Practices for Emotional Connection

In Part I—"What Organizations Miss on Today?"—we shared our research and that of other organizations that show emotional attachment is the biggest driver of business value for organizations. At the same time though, when you ask customers what they want, they would most likely tell you rational things such as competitive prices and reliability of products. Emotions would hardly even be mentioned as important aspects by customers despite them being the main driving force for customer attitudes and behavior. In Chapter 4 we even tried to explain the underlying reason behind emotions being customers' main driving force and yet them not realizing it. Now that we've shared overwhelming evidence that emotions are the key drivers of business value we will turn our attention to what it all means organizations should do.

All evidence suggests that the current practices of most organizations lead them to miss the biggest driver of business value. Just as basketball, soccer, lacrosse, and many other sports use shooting drills practices to improve their aim at the target, organizations should change their practices in order to unearth and harness the power of emotions.

In Part II, "What Organizations Need to Do Tomorrow—The Seven Business Practices for Emotional Connection," we will share advice on what organizations can do to approach the creation of an emotional attachment with customers as a science and a strategy, and how to avoid being deceived by what customers say they want.

In Chapter 5, "Practice 1: Aim Your Design on Building an Emotional Connection and a Feeling of a Relationship With Customers," we will share advice and tips on how organizations should approach the design of an emotionally engaging experience. We will look into Standford d.School's approach to design as well as our behavioral journey mapping methodology. Ideally, the focus of the organization in the design of the experience should be on aspects that would drive the most value, so in Chapter 6, "Practice 2: Take Into Account That Customers Are Not Aware of Their Inner Drivers," we would look at how organizations can avoid being deceived by what customers say they want and find the true drivers of customer behavior and attitudes. In our research we found that emotions account for almost 50 percent of business value and therefore in Chapter 7, "Practice 3: Include Emotions in Your Research," we will discuss how organizations can measure emotions in the offline and online world. Measuring emotions is one thing, but embedding them in the experience is another. In Chapter 8, "Practice 4: Be Deliberate About the Emotions You Want to Evoke and How to Evoke Them," we will share what leading organizations are doing to equip their staff with skills to evoke the targeted emotions.

Now, if emotions are key to personal and business relationships, are they the key for employee engagement too? In Chapter 9, "Practice 5: Aim for the Same Emotions in the Employee Experience," we will look into the various research on what really drives employee engagement and will share some of the key emotions to form your employee engagement strategy around. Working on both customer experience and employee experience would give you exponential benefits if it is part of an overall strategy. So in Chapter 10, "Practice 6: Make Your Customer Experience Program Sustainable," we will discuss the ingredients of a successful customer experience strategy. Heads up! One of those key ingredients is breaking down the silos between brand, product management, customer experience, and the various departments. From our research, we already found that "Brand & advertising" is one of the biggest driving factors of emotional attachment. Therefore, in Chapter 11, "Practice 7: Aim Your Brand on Making an Emotional Connection," we will look at how organizations can develop deeper emotional bonds with customers through brand and advertising and we will share some fascinating research on the role of emotions in advertising. We are also at the point of a generational shift and so we will discuss what that means for organizations and how to connect with the new generation of customers.

CHAPTER 5

Practice 1

Aim Your Design on Building an Emotional Connection and a Feeling of a Relationship With Customers

Managers should be asking themselves what they would do differently if they were to charge admission
—Joseph Pine II and James Gilmore

The evidence is vivid! Emotional attachment is the key driver of business value and yet organizations are not pursuing it with a systematic approach. In this chapter, we will share some frameworks and tips about how organizations can have a systematic approach to designing an emotionally engaging experience.

Design for Emotion

Doug Dietz's eyes fill up with tears every time he talks about one of the most emotional moments in his professional life. Doug Dietz is an industrial designer, working for GE Healthcare for more than 20 years. He had just finished a two-year project on designing a new MRI machine, when he went to see one of the first machines he had been working on, being installed in a hospital. He was in his "proud papa" mood, talking to the machine technician at the hospital when a patient came for a scan and the technician asked him to step out for a moment.

What followed was a life-changing event for Doug. In his infamous TED talk, [1] he tells the story of seeing a little girl, about 7 years old, who is weeping, walking down the hallway with her parents. "Remember, we have talked about this, you can be brave," says her father. When the little girl walks into the MRI room with her parents, Doug sees the room and the machine from a whole new perspective. On the wall you have that yellow warning sign sticker, the flooring, and everything looks "bleached out" and the room itself is "kind of dark and has those flickering fluorescent lights," he says. This is the same room he had been standing in. Doug sees the machine that he designed in a new light as well—it looks to him like "a brick with a hole in it."

So when the little girl walks into the room, she starts to cry. This has implications for hospitals as well. They have to routinely sedate pediatric patients for their scans because they are so scared that they can't lie still long enough. As many as 80 percent of pediatric patients have to be sedated. [2] Not only does this mean costs associated with the anesthesiologist's time but it means that while they are waiting for the patient to be sedated, the machine is not utilized. A lower utilization rate, while the cost of the machine and the leasing remain constant, means lower ROI and income for the hospital. And in the event that an anesthesiologist isn't available, the scan has to be postponed and the families have to go through the same process all over again.

The big problem in this story is "fear." Fear is an emotion (and a powerful one). So they have to redesign the experience to address this emotion. The reason so many patients feel fear is because their brains pick up what we would call subconscious signals: the yellow warning signs (which bring associations with the nuclear warning sign and police crime tapes), the bleached floors (smell of hospital), the flickering lights, and so on. As Doug tells in his TED talk, some kids say these things remind them of a dentist visit—not a good memory for a kid.

Doug sought advice from colleagues, and his boss at GE recommended him to visit the Stanford d.School's design-thinking workshop. I first came across their design framework in 2013 when we were working with a client in Boulder, CO. Stanford d.School's approach to design has five stages:

1. *Empathy*: Putting yourself in the shoes of the customer to really understand their needs (including unmet needs), their emotions,

desires, and how they get value from the product, service, and experience.

2. *Define*: Once you've really felt the experience from the customer perspective, you can define your problem statement (i.e., what is the problem you want to solve or the opportunity for improvement/innovation).

3. *Ideate*: Brainstorm and cocreate solutions for your problem statement.

4. *Prototype*: Create short, easily iterative storyboards or mock-ups about your solutions.

5. *Test*: Test your solutions with customers and if need be, go back to the drawing board, either back to the beginning, that is, the empathy stage, or to the ideation or prototyping stage to make amendments.

Doug followed Standford d.School's design-thinking framework to address the feeling of fear. He "went to the source" and observed how "customers," that is, kids play. He and his team couldn't help but notice the wild child imagination who could see castles in three chairs and a blanket and imagine themselves driving a train. They brainstormed what they could do with this imagination and came up with the Adventure Series™.

One of the hospital rooms that they redesigned was called "Jungle Adventure." As kids are coming in from the hallway they see some "rocks" painted on the floor and start to jump from rock to rock. As they get into the room, they hear the sound of a waterfall; they smell water with a bit of lavender (part of aromatherapy), see a light blue sky and a waterfall cascading down. The table, where they have to lay down for the scan, lowers down into the water and looks like a hollowed-out canoe. The kids are then told that this is a boat and they have to hold still so "they don't rock the boat" and if they really hold still the fish will start jumping over the boat. You don't have to have a child's wide imagination to imagine how the kids then freeze like statues.

Another room that Doug and his team designed was called "Pirate Adventure." The room is painted like a pirate ship and there is a big wooden captain's wheel that surrounds the round opening of the chamber of the MRI scanner. As the kids come in, they walk "on the dock" and see a shipwreck and sandcastles in the corner. Children are being told that they will be sailing inside the pirate ship and they have to stay completely still while on the boat. They used aromatherapy here too to "tickle all senses." In this case, they used pina colada to inject some scents into the room.

With the new design, the number of pediatric patients needing to be sedated was reduced dramatically. This of course meant that the utilization rate of these costly machines improved drastically, meaning more revenue for the hospitals. Patient satisfaction scores went up 90 percent. If you listen to Doug's TED talk, he also talks about how the hospital staff felt. Seeing kids being happy makes them feel happy as well. Thus this brings benefits to employee engagement as well.

The design of the rooms aiming to engage almost all senses reminds me of a TED talk from Jinsop Lee "Design for All 5 Senses." [3] Jinsop evaluates experiences according to how much they tickle the five senses (sight, touch, smell, sound, taste). For example, riding a bike scores 5/5 on sight, touch, and sound, not so well on smell (if you are riding in the city, chances are you'd smell mostly gasses from the car exhaust systems) and zero on taste. Contrast that with sex where almost all senses are tickled to the maximum, which, according to Jinsop, explains "why sex is so good even when it's bad" (I love this phrase). The point for me is, when you are designing an experience, think about all the senses. And when you start doing that you'll find that there is a lot of science about designing for the ears, for the smell, and so on.

I'd finish Doug's story with the tale he tells of a little girl who came over and pulled her mother's skirt. "Mommy," she asked, "can we come back tomorrow?" At this point, tears filled Doug's eyes again. His story is also featured in chapter 1 of David and Tom Kelley's book *Creative Confidence*. [4]

This last bit of his story, the fact that the little girl wants to come over again, reminds me of Joseph Pine II and James Gilmore's HBR article "Welcome to the Experience Economy" [5] where they say "managers should be asking themselves what they would do differently if they were to charge admission." This might be a bit too stretched for where most business mindsets are but that's the point. It gives a new meaning to the word experience in the mindset of managers.

The Stanford d.School design framework immediately resonated with me, as without knowing it we had been following a very similar approach, although not so rigorously defined and not having such a nice graphic as the Stanford d.School. The stamp of Stanford d.School on it also gave it more weight as a sign of "social proof," so I full-heartedly adopted the framework in my work with clients.

We've been doing the empathy stage by doing what we call "Customer Mirrors," which depending on whether it's a B2C or B2B setting is a mixture of us being the customer and walking the experience, observing customer interactions, and doing customer interviews. Just as Doug Dietz had found out, one of my biggest learnings has been that there is nothing like leaving the office to observe and go through the experience yourself. I'll tell you some of the most memorable stories to illustrate my point.

The first story comes from my colleagues who many years ago were engaged to go through the auto-claim insurance journey. One of the questions my colleagues had to figure out was "how do you safely crash a car?" Do you reverse it into a wall? In this case, you risk damaging the wall and extra litigation costs. Do you drive it into a tree? But you don't want to hurt the tree either. So they ended up going into a forest and reversing the car into a tree stump. This is where the real story starts. When they called the insurance company number, the first question they were asked was a dry "what's your policy number" (rather than are you safe and OK). Next, when a tow truck arrived, the driver (a contractor) said their policy stated that he had to drive my colleague to his home, which in that case was 150 miles away, rather than to our office which was just 5 miles away. Eventually, my colleague succeeded in talking the tow-truck driver to leave him in the office and upon being dropped off asked the driver for some piece of evidence that his car is with the insurance company. After all, the car costs a considerable amount of money. The driver then thought for a second, reached inside his truck, and tore up a piece of paper from his McDonald's meal, and wrote the car plate number and his mobile number (allegedly omitting one digit, which rendered that number useless). The team also went through a home insurance claim, for which they had to rent and flood an apartment (with the knowledge of the landlord of course). The culmination of that story was when the insurance agent, upon appearing at the flooded apartment, offered to take my colleague to an ATM machine to withdraw money to cover the excess fee on the policy as he did not have that much cash on him.

I have encountered quite a few jaw-dropping stories myself. Working with an earth-moving machine manufacturer, we visited a number of their dealerships in different countries to observe the experience of delivering a new machine to a customer. In India, upon entering their dealership, we were immediately impressed with the look of the dealership, which was a result of a "facilities project," done under the supervision of one of the regional managers accompanying us. You see a nicely laid-out exhibition machine, standing on top of a pavement consisting of small pebbles embedded in cement. It looked nice. However, when "the customer" is invited to see and inspect the machine, what we saw was a group of gentlemen in business attire walking across the dealership to the end of their premises where you can hardly find a piece of dry soil amidst the many puddles as that is the place where they wash the machines with pressured water. You also see jumper cables to the side, which they use to charge the battery and start the machine. Finally, after all this effort and preparation of the machine, we saw the delegation leave after looking at the machine's serial number. We asked where that "customer delegation" was going and we were told they were going to look for another machine with a more "lucky" serial number.

In China, we saw this brilliantly engineered machine getting stuck being offloaded from a lorry because a six-sigma project found that they can cut costs by reducing the amount of fuel they carry in the machines. So the dealer representatives came in with gas cans and started adding gasoline to the machine. Of course, any of you who have emptied a full bottle of water know that when you do this at full capacity you risk spilling it, which is exactly what was going on, while the sales representative, who sold his first machine, was having a smoke not far from the scene. In Saudi Arabia, we witnessed the machine being delivered with a manual in part-English-part-Chinese and so on....

Working with an international financial services company, we saw their most high-value and time-pressed customers being asked to complete the same information (name, e-mail, address, and phone number) on multiple nicely designed brochures (i.e., one for Hilton Honors scheme, one for Hertz's Gold Plus rewards scheme, one for Starwood's Preferred Guest scheme, etc.). This certainly didn't feel like the most thought-through design for wealthy and time-pressed individuals....

So there is nothing like seeing and going through the experience first-hand! It is so much different than what's on the process chart. There are all the things that your conscious and subconscious picks; you have all these thoughts running in the back of your mind, all those emotions....

So that "empathy" step at the beginning of Stanford d.School's frame-work is very important. The other thing that I like a lot about their frame-work is that it ends with "test." So many times, when we do our "Customer Mirrors" empathy piece, we find that the company knew about many of the problematic parts of the experience and had tried to address some in the past but for one reason or another, the solution did not work. Such was the case when we worked with the frequent-purchase loyalty rewards scheme of one of the global airline groups. After having been customers for a while, as well as doing our Emotional Signature research and qualitative research with customers, we sat down with the executive team. When we started going through our findings, for many of them, the managing direc-tor (MD) turned to one of the other directors and said "didn't we do some-thing about this two years ago?" The answer typically was "yes we did, but so and so didn't work out." Well, guess what, just because the solution didn't work out, the problem did not go away. Only that this time, after hearing some more jaw-dropping stories, the management team was resolute on seeing the changes through.

One of those jaw-dropping stories was around personalization. Upon signing, I was asked to provide a lot of personal information and infor-mation about my preferences "so they can customize the experience for me and provide me with tailored offerings." I had duly followed the pro-cess only to receive one day in my mailbox the message "Zhecho, enjoy family breaks near you" with a picture of a man and a woman holding hands with a happily jumping child. The only thing was that I had told them I didn't have a child at the time and at that point, I didn't even have a girlfriend. This coincided with two more pieces of evidence. One was another similar anecdotal story, only that this time they had sent an offer for a budget hotel to a wealthy celebrity, who they had among their mem-bers. The other piece of evidence came from our Emotional Signature quantitative research, which showed that "personalized communications and offers" would drive a lot of engagement and spend with the loyalty scheme. Upon seeing the evidence about what the experience really looks like, the MD stopped all outgoing communications, signed off with her management team 21 initiatives (some quick, straightforward changes; others more complex solutions), created a cross-functional team, and gave them the task to spend $800K in the next three months to implement the initiatives. It turned out that spending $800K in three months was not such an easy task but they risked losing the funding if they did not use the money by the end of the year. One of the success stories of that project was indeed the noticeable improvement in the relevance of communications sent to customers, which drove higher the opening rate of e-mails, offer subscriptions, and engagement with the scheme.

So, empathy and seeing the experience in the field, firsthand, can be very powerful.

How do we go about creating an emotional engagement? In Doug Dietz's story, they turned a problem and a negative emotion—fear—into a positive one. However, in many instances, the experiences are just bland. Neither particularly good, neither bad; just meeting expectations. In this case, it's not really a problem that an organization needs to work on but an opportunity to create an emotional connection (design-thinking framework would still call this a "problem statement"). One such example that stands out for me is Barclays Bank in the United Kingdom.

In 2012, at a time when the reputation of banks was still overshadowed by the 2008 financial crisis and subsequent revelations and amidst a debate for tougher banking regulations, Barclays Bank in the United Kingdom introduced the option to personalize your debit card with a picture of your choice free of charge. The service proved to be very popular. People chose pictures of their loved ones, their pets, memorable moments from their vacations, and so on. When the bank communicated the option to me I immediately took the opportunity. At the time I was in a distant, relatively new, love relationship with a person who is now my partner and the mother of my child. I put one of her pictures on my card, showed her the card, and told her "now I can't take another girl out for dinner." It was quite emotional for her. I guess it showed her that I'm serious about this relationship. Of course, I had other credit cards that I could use to pay for dinner but still....

These cards were also a conversation starter at pubs. It happened a couple of times that I was waiting to order at the bar along with someone else and we both had our personalized Barclays cards out, ready to pay, so occasionally we even started conversations about the subjects in the pictures.

Clearly, there are IT, production, and logistical costs involved with issuing these personalized cards to Barclays but they must have calculated that the emotional engagement created would generate a superior return on investment. For once it creates an emotional engagement with a piece of plastic provided to you by the bank and if you were to part with it, you'd feel a bigger loss. I know because when the bank communicated to me that they have to change my bank account sort-code and thus issue me a new card, my only question was "would it be with the same picture as the one I had?"

This for me is an example of something done purely for the purposes of emotional engagement, which also offers differentiation. It doesn't add any new functionality; it has some costs associated with it, but it generates an emotional engagement (and also a lot of publicity as too many customers took and shared pictures of their cards on social media, thus sharing sensitive information about their card number, instead of using the facility provided by the bank to share their card with those card details being blurred out).

Emotional Cookie

Another of my favorite stories comes from an insurance company we worked with a long time ago. They heard the concerns of a mother of a small child about pieces of the shattered glass window of her car potentially being left in the child seat, even after the clean-up job from the crew at the repair shop. So they decided to replace as a policy all child seats in cars that have been in an accident resulting in a smashed window. But that's not all. What really stood out was the teddy bear they put in the child seat. They estimated that the cost effect of this is negligible as they only have about 30 or so accidents like this in a year but they were amazed by the amount of publicity and compliments that this decision generated. This totally justified the investment from their perspective. In our work, later on, we called this the "emotional cookie" moment. This meant creating a peak experience moment. In this case, the peak was also right at the end of the experience making it even more powerful and memorable (remember the peak–end rule we discussed earlier in the book).

Journey Mapping

This takes us to journey mapping. As many organizations have shared with us what they do and what they have done with others, one of the major flaws that we see in their efforts and in the light of the findings of our research is that most organizations pay superficial attention to emotions in the experience. Another major flaw is that most organizations don't look at the behavioral science heuristics that could be affecting the experience but we'll come back to this one later.

Almost all customer journey maps have some sort of an indication about how the experience feels to the customer, be it a graph with ups and downs or positive or negative smile emojis. Some journey maps also feature emotions. The missed opportunities here are that these tend to be at a very superficial level and most importantly, the new experience design or the new initiatives are not really oriented toward designing for emotional engagement. Let's talk about these in turn.

People don't know what they don't know! Of course, right? Only that I find this phrase very profound when we talk about customer experience. The phrase "customer experience" sounds easy enough and besides, everyone is a customer anyway, so many people think they know what customer experience is but in reality there is a lot of science to it (check the Dunning–Kruger effect). So while we at Beyond Philosophy have been talking and thinking about emotions for years, we found that in reality, most people's vocabulary of emotions that come immediately to mind is pretty limited.

We've done workshops with employees from organizations where we map the journey customers go through with their organization and ask them to put down the customer's actions, expectations, and emotions. When it comes to writing down the emotions, most would use a very basic vocabulary, that is, happy, unhappy, pissed off, confused, and would even put lots of things that are not emotions per se. We have done this all over the United States, the United Kingdom, parts of Europe, the Middle-East, Africa, and all the way to China. Hardly anyone would write things like valued, appreciated, cared for, or indulged unprompted. So we found the need to prompt participants to use a larger vocabulary of emotions and we displayed the pyramid of emotions (Figure 1.1) during the emotions exercise. In fact, when I was leading a number of journey mapping workshops in China, I had forgotten about this, and it was our Chinese partners that pointed out to me that people struggle to name emotions. I said "of course, my bad" and immediately pointed them to our solution for this problem (i.e., displaying Figure 1.1 during the exercise).

This "solution" though only addresses the "hypothesis" of what customers feel in the experience as here we talk about company employees trying to map out how customers feel. One might question the benefits of such exercise but, if you do some, you'd find many things you haven't thought of. We always get amazed how people with great knowledge of the processes, who have been with the company for 20+ years, get surprised to learn about a process customers go through with credit control, a number of cold transfers at the contact center, a promise from the sales representatives, a favor customers ask from account managers, and so on. Whenever people from various departments join for this type of exercise there are always moments of "oh, I didn't know we were doing that" or "I'm not quite sure what exactly happens next." There are also a lot of dead-ends in the process where the organization realizes the customer would never come back. I remember in one of the first mapping sessions that I did many years ago with the employees from the B2B division of a U.S. telecom when one of the employees said "next thing that will happen is that we'll call the customer back." Then another one countered, "No we won't, look at this customer's profile, he only spends $30 with us, he'll never get a call from us in a million years." For us, as outside consultants, this serves several purposes. We develop a more detailed understanding of what customers go through. This allows us to divide the experience into several key journey moments that we need to cover when we interview customers and we are equipped with some hypotheses to test. Most importantly, though, employees can tell us about internal policies and other "inside" things that affect the customer experience that customers won't be aware of as those were happening "behind the scenes." This way we found that a company we were working with, which supplies pubs and restaurants with beer and drinks, had a credit policy that they would allow customers to order up to a point based on the average of the last three months of transactions. However, when spring comes and people storm the pub gardens to enjoy the sun with a beer in hand, this policy was woefully inadequate because January, February, and March are usually slow business months for pubs.

A byproduct of this exercise is that employees start to think about the actual experience customers go through not just with them but also with competitors, as oftentimes, when a prospect contacts a company, they contact two or three other companies as well. They also start to think about the customer's emotions and what causes these emotions.

We have found a number of benefits coming out from a customer journey mapping session with employees, but still, that only gives us the "hypothesis" of the customer's experience and emotions. To understand the true emotions customers feel, one has to "walk the experience" as much as possible, interview customers and dig down deeper to find the underlying causes for their emotions and attitudes, conduct quantitative customer research to find what aspects of the experience and emotions drive or destroy value for the organization, and so on. This will create a much deeper and accurate understanding of the actual emotions customers feel in the experience and which of them drive or destroy the most value. When the experience is predominantly or entirely digital, then using facial emotion recognition tools is a good way to authentically measure the different emotions customers feel along the journey (we discuss the various ways to get insights and measure customer emotions in Chapter 7).

The second problem with how organizations do journey mapping relates to the ideation sessions and designing the new experience. Even though they may have considered how the experience feels from a customer's perspective and some emotions, typically the new initiatives that they come up with are not really oriented toward designing for an emotional engagement. The mindset for most organizations is such that they focus on resolving the issues and not so much on thinking about how to make customers feel appreciated for being a customer and for the tenure of the relationship, making customers feel cared for, and so on. Typically, the customer journey mapping process will uncover a number of issues in the experience. Those are where the experience falls through the organizational cracks and fails to meet customer expectations. Understandably organizations look at how to fix those and improve the experience. I, myself, in working with some organizations might have been guilty of that as well. I caught myself being guilty of that when I reviewed the topics for ideation that we had prepared on the basis of the journey mapping project we were doing with a hospital. When I reviewed the topics I realized that they were all about fixing issues/subpar experiences that we had found along the journey. Fixing the issues is like working on the negative emotions. You can reduce those but that doesn't mean that the positive emotions will automatically go up (i.e., customers starting to feel more valued, cared for, pleased, happy, etc.). Once I realized that I included a couple of extra topics for ideation. We pitched the idea of an "emotional cookie" moment (i.e., a "teddy bear"-like moment, as described in the insurance company story earlier on). Since, in this case, we were looking at a neuroscience journey, often involving multiple visits, surgery, and postsurgery rehabilitation therapies, the hospital team fully embraced the idea. We called it an "emotional cookie: making experiences memorable for certain patients by triggering positive emotions (i.e., moments of surprise, care, etc.)."

Design the Peak–End

Since that moment of realization when working with the hospital team, we also made it a practice to incorporate Kahneman's peak–end rule in the design of experiences. What this meant in practice is that where customers might feel is the peak of their experience, that is, signing a mortgage contract and getting the keys to their new house or getting a brand new bulldozer machine, there will be a deliberately designed peak moment to commemorate the experience, while at the same time we'll do a deliberate design for the endings: the endings to meetings, the ending of a mortgage contract, of the machine leasing or insurance protection plan, and so on.

When we started designing for the endings we found that it is a much overlooked area of the experience. Think about for a moment how many times it happens to you that you have some interaction with a business where you are giving them some information, you pay for the service, and you are left hanging at the end not completely sure whether you are all done, what happens next, what the timelines are, and so on. Being cursed with knowledge about what a good ending should look like, I find myself quite often in these situations. So working with the financial arm of an earth-moving equipment manufacturer, we asked them to map what the ending of the machine protection plan looks like and we found that not much was happening. We pointed out to them that the moment an expensive machine runs out of insurance coverage is clearly a great sales opportunity to replace the machine with a new one, extend the coverage, or sign a service deal. Working with a bank we found again that not much was happening at the end of the mortgage period. Because most mortgage contracts are for 10, 15, or even 30 years, the bank staff never really gave much thought to it. However, at any given moment there are many customers whose mortgages expire, and given that they will now have extra freed-up buying power those will be great prospects for a second home mortgage, a new car lease, a new consumer loan, and so on. The next thing was that there is a portion of customers who pay up the mortgage ahead of time and in a 10-year period may do two or more mortgage deals, so designing a memorable "end" experience offers a number of economic benefits as well. When you think of endings, you shouldn't only be thinking about the end of the customer journey but also about creating a deliberate "ending ceremony" for each customer interaction, for each key journey step, and so on.

Show You Know Customers

One of the ways to create emotional engagement and a feeling of a relationship is by showing your customers that you "know" them. This is particularly important when it comes to digital experiences but shouldn't be neglected in the human-to-human interactions either. After all, you can't have a relationship with someone you don't know, right? Remember what Harry Reis had found to be one of the key pillars for personal relationships: understanding, that is, "my partner knows me and what is important to me."

Over my time working with organizations I have found this to be one of the key drivers of feeling a relationship with the organization and business value. I think I first started to notice this and to think about it when I saw the simple but brilliant "Member Since" printed on the American Express cards. We knew it had a big effect on their cardmembers. For customers, it was a thing of pride and recognition for being loyal customers. Just as I'm writing these lines I googled it so I don't just base this argument on my own opinion and guess what you can see in the top results? "We know card members seem to have this affinity for their member-since date," says the company's VP of social media communications in a 2013 *PRWeek* article [6] and then I see a customer saying he's thinking about canceling his card but has "been a member for a very long time, and thus chuckle when I see the 'Member Since' date on my card," [7] he writes in a forum.

Fast forward to the present day; the customers of a Canadian company supplying commercial customers with heating oil and propane are complaining that they used to order through the local offices but for a period of time, the company changed it so customers had to call a central 1-800 number to order delivery. When you read between the lines you see that by doing this the company has taken away the feeling of a relationship with the local representatives who knew them, knew where their business was located, and so on. One customer says that the problem is not that the receptionist is a bad receptionist (that's what the customer calls the call center staff that answers the call) but that they have no knowledge of the local area, no records are kept, and they have to repeat the directions every time. This doesn't create a feeling of relationship and customer loyalty, does it?

Talking about keeping records reminds me of the work we did with a water utility company in the United Kingdom. We had conducted our Emotional Signature research and "knows me as a customer and past history" was one of the key drivers of value as well as aspects related to issue resolution. When we went with the crews to see what's actually happening on the ground, visiting customers who have reported issues, we saw that the notes in their CRM system on the customer account were ordered from oldest to newest. The crews had tablets but they were slow and oftentimes working in remote areas with bad or no connectivity. Furthermore, sometimes they said they had to go through nine pages to get to the latest notes on what the customer had reported. This meant that oftentimes the crew didn't appear to "know the customer and their past history." What was even worse, when customers were not around to talk to the crews it was common that the actual issue would not be fixed which resulted in extra costs for bringing the crews back to the site. As I've said earlier in the book, there's nothing like observing the experience firsthand.

There is also research that provides further evidence about the effect of recognizing customer's past interactions. Researchers at the Corporate Executive Board (CEB), now a subsidiary of Gartner, called it "baggage handling." They studied customer calls in a contact center and found that the ratings customers give following an interaction are greatly influenced by the memory of their previous interactions (remember the peak–end rule we spoke about earlier in the book). They called the customer's memory of previous interactions with the organization their "baggage." The thing is that call center reps had the tendency to avoid addressing this past "baggage" as it could be uncomfortable and difficult to handle. But do customers want to have their "baggage" to be acknowledged? The CEB team ran an experiment [8] in a call center, where agents were randomly assigned to either ignore the previous interactions (issues) the customer had with the call center or acknowledge them. Imagine a rep saying "Oh, I see you've called before about this problem. Tell us what happened so we can try something new" and another saying "I understand you are having a problem" and then go through the same usual script of problem fixing. The results from the experiment showed that customers whose call history was acknowledged rate the agent almost twice as high as the other and the perceived effort on their part to resolve the problem was down by 84 percent. [9] Effective baggage handling also resulted in 48 percent increase in the Customer Interaction Outcome Index, which is a compilation of several common customer metrics including customer effort, customer satisfaction, NPS®, and quality of service.

Charles Duhigg, a *New York Times* bestselling author, shares another very interesting example about the power of showing you know customers in his book *The Power of Habit* (2012). He tells the story of how YMCA (often referred to as the Y), one of the United States' largest nonprofit organizations with more than 1,600 gyms and community centers, hired a social scientist and a statistician to figure out how to make people more engaged with their programs and exercise more. At the time the conventional wisdom at the executive level was that people wanted fancy exercise equipment and modern facilities. Bill Lazarus and Dean Abbott analyzed the data from more than 150,000 YMCA member satisfaction surveys gathered through the years and found that while facilities' attractiveness and the availability of fitness equipment were key to sign up members, what got people to stick was something else. "Retention, the data said was driven by emotional factors, such as whether employees knew member's names or said hello when people walked in." [10] It turned out that showing that you know customers and satisfying their social needs could go a long way in even making a nation healthier.

All these examples show that it's important for organizations to show that they know their customers and acknowledge past interactions. I think the underlying reasons behind this phenomenon (acknowledging customer tenure) are that customers want to feel valued and appreciated for being customers and be shown the necessary respect that comes with that. All these are emotions that our research found to be big drivers of value for organizations.

The psychology of feeling respect is an interesting one by itself. Professors Yuen J. Huo and Kevin R. Binning from the University of California write in their paper that,

> the experience of respect matters to people because it reflects two core motives of social life—the striving for status (recognition as a worthy contributor to the group) and the need to belong (formation of meaningful, affiliative bonds with other group members).[11]

Remember the American Express "Member Since?" This explains why it's so powerful from a psychological perspective. They say that "respect from the group shapes social engagement, self-esteem, and health." Therefore showing you know customers, addressing their "baggage," and equipping agents with the skills to evoke the feeling of respect should definitely be part of your training manual.

Take the Experience to an Extra Level Through Personalization

Another way to show customers that you "know" them is through personalization. One can even argue that that's going even further. However, personalization is no longer a "nice to do" thing anymore. Customers are expecting it, looking for it, and shopping more where they get it. According to a Google/Ipsos survey, over half of U.S. consumers say they are interested in seeing personalized content when shopping. [12] What is also important to note from that research is that customers say they are comfortable sharing their information as long as they feel like they're getting value in return.

I remember interviewing customers of a large financial company with charge cards all the way back to 2011. They were expecting to receive personalized offers because in their mind the organization was clearly able to see when, where, and what they spent money on. However, the organization at the time didn't have the capability to do much with the data and on top of that, they thought people would be more worried about the privacy of their information.

Clearly, privacy is a major concern for many customers but numerous research also suggests that people are willing to share information as long as they believe the organization will use it in a safe and ethical way to remove friction and make their experience more positive and helpful. Customers are looking to save time, find the right product for them without digging too much for it, and also get a discount or at least some appreciation for being a loyal customer (this is where loyalty programs come in).

As we've shown multiple times in this book, the fact that customers say they want something doesn't mean it's something that will drive value for the organization so I'd just mention another finding from Google/ BCG research. Customers rated retailers providing highly personalized experiences 20 percent higher on NPS*. [13] Bain & Company's data also shows that leaders in providing personalized experience have two to three times higher conversion rates and get a 5 to 10 percent uplift in sales compared to control groups. [14]

When we talk about personalization, clearly Amazon has been the leader in this field for many years and other retailers are trying to mimic part of what they do. Amazon is great at showing relevant products when you come back. They were also the ones to start showing "frequently bought together" and "related products." Shortly prior to my son's birth, I purchased from Amazon a baby monitor and a couple of other baby items. Soon I started getting e-mails from Amazon Family with the title

"Your 12 week old," "Your 4 Month Old," "Your 5 Month Old," all the way till "18 month old." I don't recall signing for them at all, but nevertheless I found them incredibly relevant (I seem to have opened about six of them). I remember the first ones I received as coming with great toy ideas and other very relevant items. I wasn't at all surprised that they have figured out that I've become a father as I remember another story featured in Charles Dugigg's book *The Power of Habit*. The story is about how Target found a girl was pregnant even before her father did. [15] Target's in-house statistician Andrew Pole was tasked to figure out pregnant customers so they can target them early on with relevant products and almost keep them as customers for life. Pole looked at historical buying data for women who had signed up for Target baby registries in the past and found about 25 products that could indicate whether or not a woman is likely to be pregnant and even in which trimester of their pregnancy they are likely to be. Equipped with the knowledge of which customers are likely to be expecting a child, Target began to send them relevant promotional materials with coupons for discounts on diapers, lotions, and so on. That is until one day a father turned up in one of their stores complaining about these materials being sent to his daughter who was still in high school. The store manager apologized and even followed up with another call a few weeks later only that this time the father had a much different tone and said that apparently some things have been going on without his knowledge. Target learned that sending pregnancy-oriented offers may spook some customers and began to make the promotions look random by mixing baby products with things pregnant women are unlikely to buy, that is, diapers next to wine glasses, baby clothes next to lawnmowers, and so on.

Lately, Amazon sent me a list of recommended books that align quite nicely with what I read. Most of them were about behavioral science; some were from authors I've already read. Some were books that I've already read on paper without their knowledge so it just shows how good their matches were. Again, I don't think I've signed for this type of e-mail but this must be triggered by recent searches for books on Amazon.

Other retailers have taken a more straightforward and cheaper approach by simply asking site visitors for some information so they can tailor the results for them. So, for example, a baby retailer would ask visitors if they are "expecting," "new parents," or "buying a gift," while a beauty products retailer would ask visitors to select their skin concern and they would get results of products with badges that fit their skin. This is particularly important for retailers with large catalogs of products because the sooner customers get to the products that match their needs and style the best, the more likely they are to convert.

Other retailers, such as customized jewelry retailer Gemvara, would have data showing that most customers don't make a purchase on their first visit but rather on their second or third visit. So they would try to accumulate data for you over time so that next time you visit you can pick up things where you left them, show you the products you were most interested in, or give you inspiration so you don't have to restart your journey all over again.

Whereas 5 to 10 years ago, most of this personalization was done thanks to the work by statisticians such as Andrew Pole and was following a more rules-based system, nowadays this is all moving to ML. As technology has progressed, you can put an algorithm and the tools in place to find the expected and unexpected personalizations but for those algorithms to work they require a lot of data. We'll talk more about the future of CX and the use of AI in Part III of the book.

Sometimes though, personalization is not so much about complex algorithms but about perception. The power of personalization comes from the fact that people love it when something feels made just for them. Think about your daily horoscope.

> Today is your day to shine, [put your zodiac sign you like], so give it your all. Be sure that you get the credit you deserve for all you do. Try not to fall into self-pity. Be yourself and people will naturally follow your lead.

Just how amazingly this fits you! In psychology, this is known as the Barnum effect (called after the great American showman of the 19th century, P.T. Barnum). The Barnum effect (also known as the Forer effect) is a cognitive bias where people are led to believe personality descriptions describe them well when told they specifically apply to them, despite the fact that those descriptions are general in nature and could apply to almost everyone. The American psychologist Bertram Forer once conducted an experiment and told participants that they would get unique personalized feedback if they fill this personality test. All participants were subsequently given similar generic statements but nevertheless, they rated the accuracy of the test with 4.26 (5 being most accurate). [16]

Spotify and Netflix are two other examples that make good use of this phenomenon with tailored selections of songs and movies. Spotify features "Your daily mix" right in front of you when you log in, while Netflix has a "recommended for you" and a match score for relevancy. While Spotify and Netflix may indeed use some algorithms to personalize the suggested content, according the people's preferences, the main point is that they are trying to serve a psychological need for customers, that is, that things are personalized to them.

The Emotional Design of Products, Websites, and Applications

So far, in this chapter, we mainly spoke about the design of experiences. If you are in a business where customers have to choose between your product and similar products from your competitors you have to remember the research from Antonio Damasio that we started this book with. Without emotions we, people, find it hard to decide what to wear in the morning and what to eat for lunch. As we've said earlier, people would often say that they weigh the pros and cons before making a decision, like my colleague, who was making lists about the key attributes that he wanted in a product ... and always ended up buying Sony. The reality is that we often make decisions based on how we feel (or how we expect we'll feel) and then justify those with logic.

Everything around us has been designed and, in one way or another, it stimulates an emotional response in us, whether good or bad. If you put some biological sensors on you you'll see that we experience an emotional reaction to our environment pretty much with every breath we take. And so products can drive emotional bonding with the brand as well. In fact, after I found that "Emotional attachment" was the biggest driver of value when compared to the traditional customer life cycle touchpoints most organizations use, I then reanalyzed the data to see which of the traditional customer life cycle touchpoints had the biggest effect on

"Emotional attachment." "Product & use" with 15 percent contribution came in joint third place as the biggest driver of "Emotional attachment." Of course this varies from industry to industry. We'll talk more about this part of the research in Chapter 8 (see Table 8.1).

This shouldn't come as a surprise to designer and psychologist Donald (Don) Norman, a pioneer in usability and human–computer interaction. He was one of the first to talk about emotional design in his book *Emotional Design: Why We Love (or Hate) Everyday Things* (Basic Books 2004). Because emotions and cognition work in tandem (per Damasio) as we relate to products, Norman argues that organizations should go beyond the functionality issues and accommodate aesthetic elements that appeal to consumer emotions. He suggests that there are three levels (dimensions) to emotional design, which are interconnected:

Visceral–Behavioral–Reflective

The first is the "visceral" level, which is about our first, intuitive (gut-feel), and sensory reaction to how things look, feel, smell, and sound. It is powerful and often felt at a subconscious level. We just know whether we like or not a product. Think about how you like one watch over another, one car design over another. James Dyson even made an empire out of designing aesthetically pleasing vacuum cleaners. While the fact that a more aesthetically pleasing or avant-garde design of a product such as a watch, a car, a building can command more attraction (and higher price) shouldn't come as a surprise to anyone, one has to note that this applies to the design of websites and interfaces as well. Back in the 1990s, two Japanese researchers studied two different layouts of controls for ATMs. They were interested in finding out how aesthetics affected perceived usability. Both ATM interface designs were identical in function, the number of buttons, and how they worked, but one had the buttons and screens arranged attractively, the other unattractively. Surprise! The Japanese found that the attractive ones were perceived to work better. Then an Israeli scientist, puzzled by the finding that attractiveness could actually change our perception of how something works, decided to replicate the experiment. He took the designs from the Japanese researchers, translated them into Hebrew and rerun the experiment in Israel while rigorously controlling for methodology. "Not only did he replicate the Japanese findings, but the results were stronger in Israel than in Japan, contrary to his belief that beauty and function 'were not expected to correlate,'" writes Donald Norman. [17] So it turns out that beautiful is useful! Or is it?! This may only be true until people actually get to use something that is beautiful but not particularly easy to use. In another experiment participants were asked to rate four different versions of the same online shop "differing in interface–aesthetics (low vs. high) and interface–usability (low vs. high)." They had to find specific items and then rate the shop before and after usage on perceived aesthetics and perceived usability. The results showed that the "what is beautiful is useful" notion can be reversed. In their experiment, the frustration of poor usability lowered the ratings on perceived aesthetics, while aesthetics did not affect perceived usability. [18] As we said, these three levels are interconnected. So let's talk about the next level...

The second level is the "behavioral," which is about the consumers' perception of the ease of use and functionality of products and apps. This is about intuitive way-finding and use. For example, I always found Apple products and the iOS much more intuitive since the first time I got my hands on an iPhone. My partner has had Android phones since the day I met her (nine years and counting) and to date, I still have difficulties finding my way around the interface when I need to do something. Similarly, a friend who had an iPhone for a number of years switched briefly to a Samsung only to ditch it in a short while because he found it frustrating getting used to the operating system.

The third level is "reflective." This is about our innate sense of identity through the consumption of the product. This is the highest level of emotional design, representing our conscious thought layer. For example, people might be consciously choosing to buy Patagonia clothing because they identify with their values against overconsumption just like there are people that identify with Lush because of their stance against animal cruelty and animal testing.

There are many brands that can stand out as an embodiment of these categories but I'd be brief and name just two. Apple is an embodiment of all three categories and that is probably the reason why they have so many raving fans that feel emotionally attached to the brand and their products (me included). They put a lot of thought and effort into the aesthetic design. Sometimes this even goes to the detriment of function-ality and causes angerment among some users (I'm talking about the lack of ports on the MacBook here among other things). As we've said earlier, their products are very intuitive and the many books by former employ-ees are a testament about how much thought and conscious efforts go into that. Not to mention of course that they also do the job in terms of functionality. When it comes to the reflective layer, you could also consider some of their products as fashionable items and accessories (i.e., the iWatch, the original iPad), while the iPhone could even be perceived by some as a status symbol in developing countries given the difference in price with some low-cost Asian brands. These aspects are reflective of peoples' aspires to be trendy, fashionable, and command a status. I would name BMW as the next brand embodiment of all three categories because that would take us to the next point. Similar to Apple, I, along with many others, find their products (cars, bikes, and accessories) aes-thetically designed. I remember once watching a documentary, which showed a DJ working in their factory, who tests so many different sounds in order to choose the right one for one of their buttons. I was impressed with their attention to detail and I think that this seemingly insignifi-cant short snippet of the documentary that I watched still influences my perception of them as an organization. Talking about buttons, to date I remember how I got in a rent-a-car, after landing in Toronto, Canada, and it happened to be a Ford with so many buttons on the wheel and around it that I even took a picture of it. My attention was torn between driving on unfamiliar, at the time, roads and finding the right button for the radio and climate control among the forest of buttons. Then of course, similar to Apple, one may say that BMW has the reflective emo-tional appeal as well. However, the reason I picked BMW was because of one other category as well. Personality!

Aarron Walter, another authority in the field of emotional design with a lot of practitioner experience behind his back as he was the man who founded the User Experience (UX) practice at MailChimp, talks about a personality layer. In his book *Designing for Emotion* (A Book Apart 2011), he too argues that a product has to be functional, reliable, and usable (in that order) before a layer of pleasure can be applied. Personality, he says, is the platform for emotion. "It's the framework we use to crack jokes, empathize, and connect with other humans. If we can bake emotion into the interfaces we design, we reap big benefits." [19] Just like when you interact with a person overtime you get a feeling of their personality, products (physical products, software applications, websites, etc.) can communicate emotion and personality. What creates a personality for an app, an interface, a website? A mascot people can identify your organization with can go a long way. Think of the MailChimp monkey, the Michelin Man, the M&Ms, Geico's quirky lizard, twitter's bird "Larry," and so on. Add humor or wittiness to the mascot and that makes the interaction a lot more emotional and memorable. One of the examples that Aarron Walter gives that I really like is how when you type a tweet in the Feathers app, the bird mascot that they use fills to give feedback of the message length and when you go over the limit it turns red. People fall in love with these kind of things. What other things create personality? Colors and layouts, clever copy writing and storytelling, animations, attention to detail, and so on. I'll stop here because I can't say much that is not already written in the books mentioned earlier by Dan Norman, Aarron Walter, and the authors of *Design for Emotion* (Elsevier Science 2012) Trevor van Gorp and Edie Adams.

So when I think of BMW I think of a car with a sporty soul, handling, and sound. When I think of a Mercedes I associate it with a more elegant and smooth ride. Those are the two distinct personalities that I associate those brands with. Of course, you may have a different opinion based on different experiences and learned associations. Therein lies part of what makes designing for emotion difficult.

So, designing the product for an emotional appeal is very powerful, but how do you do that? Dan Norman says that that is still an art and an intuition, while the other aforementioned authors certainly provide a number of practical tips when it comes to websites, software, and applications. What you can do, however, is to test the customer's emotional reaction and measure the customer emotions and the level of their emotional attachment with the organization. We'll look into that in the next chapter.

The important thing to note is that providing customers the feeling of a personalized experience, showing that you know them, designing products, interfaces, and experiences with emotions in mind (i.e., Doug Dietz's Adventure Series) are ways to drive business value. In our experience, we have found that applying the Stanford d.School's approach to journey mapping is a simple, cheap, and yet powerful method to review the customer journey and ideate solutions on how to improve the customer experience. As a framework it can be applied to designing digital experiences as well. When doing journey mapping, it's important to take note of the customer emotions and the behavioral science principles in play (such as the peak–end rule). Then, in the ideation process, it's easy to get fixated on the issues and the rational aspects that people brag about but the big opportunity lies in focusing on aspects that create emotional attachment. In the design of the new experience, organizations need to take into account the principles of behavioral science and think about how to methodically evoke the emotions that would drive conversion, retention, recommendation, and so on. Sometimes this ranges from witty mascots and sophisticated AI-driven algorithms to personalize the experience, while in others it is as simple as greeting customers by name. I say "simple" because it is easy to do, although it requires scaling across thousands of branches and hundreds of thousands of interactions. The biggest challenge though is actually finding that this is what would drive the most value because, if you recall the YMCA, executives were used to thinking customers want more shiny gyms. This is what we would look into in the next chapter. In Chapter 6, we would look at how organizations can avoid being deceived by what customers say they want and find the true value drivers in the experience.

Practitioner Tips From This Chapter

- Design for emotion. A useful tool is journey mapping that follows Stanford d.School's approach to design.
- The empathy phase is very important. Talking to employees with firsthand knowledge of the process and customer interactions is very helpful. Nothing compares, however, to going out and observing the experience firsthand and talking to customers in-depth about their journey. When talking to customers, beware that they may not be aware of what really drives their attitudes and behavior toward the organization and often have difficulties talking about emotions. So one has

to "peel the onion" and dig below the rational surface. The keys to success are to map the emotional experience (positive, negative, or bland), understand the root-cause drivers of those emotions, and also the behavioral science principles that affect customer behavior.

- Then again, when it comes to the ideation process for the redesign of the experience, it could be very tempting to just focus on the easy fixes for the instances the experience breaks down, but you should also think about how to embed in the design of the experience the emotions that will drive the desired customer behavior.

- Focusing your redesign on aspects of the experience that would drive the desired customer behavior may mean that you need to do research to find those drivers in the first place. We'll talk more about that in the next chapters.

- Consider how you can show that you "know" your customers and how you can personalize the experience to them because those are typically driving emotional attachment.

- Your physical products, website, application, and software interface also elicit emotional reactions, so make sure to test and measure those as well.

CHAPTER 6

Practice 2

Take Into Account That Customers Are Not Aware of Their Inner Drivers

I think because, at the end of the day, what consumers told us they would do, and what they actually did, were different things
—Simon Fox

The advice we gave in the previous chapter sounds simple enough, right? So why aren't organizations doing it? Many organizations do some form of journey mapping but as we said hardly anyone is designing methodically with customer emotions in mind. So why is that emotions are key drivers of customer behavior and consequently value for organizations?

One of the main reasons is that emotions are not flagged on organizations' radars. As we've provided examples in Chapter 2, customers don't know what they really want. They are not aware of their inner drivers. In Chapter 4, we tried to explain the psychological reasons for this phenomenon. The overwhelming evidence we provided shows that the traditional methods of research that organizations use would not flag and single out emotional aspects as value drivers and put an ROI case. In this chapter, we will look at how organizations could avoid being deceived by what customers say they want and do research that gets to the emotional and subconscious value drivers.

My observations from working with many large organizations and looking at the type of research they do with customers are that most use flawed research methods that don't provide them with the insights about the root-cause drivers of customer behavior that are needed to direct attention and investment to the aspects that would really improve customer experience and bring economic benefits to the organization. And I am not alone in this assessment. The American Customer Satisfaction Index (ACSI) data shows that customer satisfaction among major companies has mostly flattened between 2013 and 2018 and since 2019 there has been a sharp decline, which as of Q3 of 2021 stands at levels last seen in 2005. While Covid-19 certainly has something to do with it, the decline had started before that. According to the ACSI, the main reason for the long stagnation and subsequent decline is not for the lack of attention by businesses who have invested a lot of effort and resources in enhancing the customer experience. Nor do they contribute it to the lack of data either, as companies are now sitting on more data about their customers than at any point in the past. "While companies today have more data about their customers, the analytics employed to turn data into information are for the most part not good enough," [1] they say.

Many organizations do some sort of research. The most common and used approach we have seen is a two to three question survey after an interaction. This typically involves the NPS® question (or another value indicator question, be it for customer satisfaction, retention, customer effort, etc.) and an open-ended question or a question of the sort "how would you rate the interaction with the agent you spoke to?" These do a good job for tactical and tracking purposes but don't provide enough information for strategic purposes. Open-ended questions are good and we use those as well. However, we use them to find more context about the key value drivers that we have found. As we have provided data and examples earlier in the book, most people will only talk about the rational aspects (product price, etc.) and service aspects. We often see an equal amount of comments from customers saying "I like the price—it's competitive" and others saying "your pricing is way off, so and so gives me a better deal." This is not to say that verbal comments can't be analyzed, on the contrary, but the typical two to three questions survey is hardly a good fit for the purpose of setting the strategic focus with the confidence executives need.

In addition to transactional surveys, like the ones described earlier, many organizations would use slightly longer "relationship" surveys. The main issue with those is that organizations hardly include any emotional aspects in those surveys and the methods they use for analysis. Typically, at the start of our work with organizations they would share with us the research that they have done (oftentimes using outside vendors). Most of the analysis that we have seen has been based on correlation. The thing is though that correlation is not causation. One of our favorite stories is about a small port town where residents noticed that as the seagulls fill the town, lots of local women get pregnant. So you could correlate the two but, of course, what was truly happening is that the seagulls were following the fishing boats where sailors were gutting the fish on their way home. Regardless of how many times you hear the phrase "correlation does not imply causation," it still bemuses people to find some strange relationships. Tyler Vigen is one of those and has created a series of comical charts that show "spurious correlations." [2] My favorite among her selection is that the number of people who died by becoming tangled in their bedsheets correlates with the amount of revenue generated by skiing facilities in the United States. Sara Silverstein, on the other side, tells the Business Insider audience that the percentage of obese children in each state correlates with the searches for Prince's song Purple Rain lyrics.[3] Regression and, even better, multiple regression are much better forms of statistical analysis but then again those don't include path analysis (in other words, finding causal relationships, i.e., root-cause drivers). A more advanced form of statistical analysis, for the purposes we talk about, is using SEM and in particular partial least squares (PLS) path modeling. This is what we use. I was thinking of not boring you with details about statistics here (I've fallen asleep multiple times reading about it) but since we like to base what we do on science, I'd just mention a few things.

There are many academic references about SEM and PLS but I'd just quote a paper that has sat in my library since 2009 by researchers Jörg Henseler (now a professor at the University of Twente), Christian M. Ringle (now a professor at the Hamburg University of Technology), and Rudolf R. Sinkovics (now a professor at the University of Auckland). They cite researchers that say "SEM has become *de rigueur* in validating instruments and testing linkages between constructs," while also noting that PLS has been used by a growing number of researchers from various disciplines such as strategic management, e-business, organizational behavior, consumer behavior, and marketing. [4] Their research found that by 2008, more than 20 studies using PLS had been published in five top-tier marketing journals and more than 30 articles on international marketing using PLS were published in double-blind reviewed journals. Its growing popularity among researchers is attributed to the fact that it's well suited for prediction-oriented research and exploratory modeling. Among the advantages of using PLS that the authors note is the fact that it's methodologically advantageous when it comes to complex models. This is one of the things we like about it. The world is complex, a customer has multiple touchpoints of interaction with an organization, and there are multiple aspects of each interaction (e.g., the functional side, the experiential aspect). So we build a complex model where we have the various aspects of the experience grouped in a number of touchpoints. Those are then linked to several groupings of positive and negative emotions and with indicators of value for the organization (e.g., spend, likelihood to remain a customer, likelihood to recommend). This way we end up with a model with many variables and constructs and PLS is well suited to handle the calculations. The advancements in computer power also help in this regard.

Another characteristic of the PLS path modeling that makes it well suited for marketing and customer experience research is that it allows the computation of cause–effect relationship models that employ both "reflective" and "formative" measurement models. Most common in research is reflective models where, in simple terms, all measures are reflective of the construct (latent variable is the statistics term). That means measures are representative of the variable. For example, reflective indicators of satisfaction with a hotel are attributes like "I like this hotel," "I am looking forward to staying in this hotel," and "I recommend this hotel." Reflective measures are interchangeable and should be highly correlated with one another. On the other hand, when you construct a formative model, each aspect represents a different dimension of the construct. So in a formative model about satisfaction with hotel accommodation, you would have attributes like "friendliness of personnel," "cleanliness of rooms," and "quality of fitness equipment." This type is more useful to us. When we build formative models we can find the weighting of each dimension (attribute) in the construct. So, for example, among the attributes of the

"Customer service" touchpoint in the model for one oil and gas company, we had "ability to resolve issue upon first contact." It had the highest importance score among the attributes in the touchpoint but was only contributing to 36 percent of the value of that touchpoint, while "support staff treat me as a valuable member" was the least desired but with 43 percent it had the highest contribution to the value of the touchpoint construct. Similarly, we could say that "accuracy of delivery" had three times more contribution to the value of the "delivery" touchpoint than "timeliness of delivery," even though the latter was deemed more important by customers.

Another favorable characteristic of PLS is that it can be used to estimate path models when sample sizes are small. This is particularly useful when we work with B2B organizations who do not have many hundreds or thousands of customers in a particular segment or where it would be very difficult and costly to get a large sample size (e.g., active decision makers for laboratory diagnostics or decision makers for construction companies who rent excavators).

Doing conjoint analysis and focus groups research with customers are two other commonly used forms of research that could result in misleading directions, missed opportunities, and even big losses. This is not to say that there is no use in these forms of research. We use some variations of them as well but one should remember that, as the famous David Oglivy's quote goes: "Consumers don't think how they feel. They don't say what they think and they don't do what they say." People are very good at coming up with answers when asked for their thoughts and feelings though.

Take, for example, the Trinity Mirror's *New Day* newspaper which launched in the United Kingdom in February 2016 and closed down in May the same year, less than three months after launch. Why? According to the publisher's chief executive: because consumers did not want what they said they wanted. Following market research on what readers might want, *New Day* set out to be a positive, politically neutral newspaper. It turned out that's not what customers actually wanted.

Asked why the daily title did not succeed, Simon Fox told City A.M.: "I think because, at the end of the day, what consumers told us they would do, and what they actually did, were different things." [5]

Then there is Tropicana's 2009 infamous packaging redesign failure. The PepsiCo-owned brand, which is the market leader in North America with sales over $700M, decided to change the packaging for the North American market of its best-selling and most notary product, the Tropicana Orange Juice. They had entrusted the work on both the campaign and the packaging to a marketing agency they had worked previously with and also lined up a $35M advertising campaign that prominently featured the new packaging. I am sure that before the launch they must have had some research with customers given the budget allocated to this campaign but whatever people had said beforehand it must have been very different to what people actually did at the supermarket shelves.

Soon after the launch, consumers started criticizing the new design, especially on social networks. Two months later, sales dropped by 20 percent, and this spectacular decrease in sales represented a loss of $30M for Tropicana. [6] At the same time sales of competitors increased by double-digits, benefiting from Tropicana's debacle and showing that the decline is not due to suddenly people consuming less orange juice.

Neil Campbell, president at Tropicana North America in Chicago, part of PepsiCo Americas Beverages, explains their decision to revert back to the "old" design, about a month and a half after the launch of the campaign. He says that they changed it not because they saw complaints in social media—the number of those has only been a fraction of a percent of their user base—but because the criticism came from their most loyal customers. "We underestimated the deep emotional bond they had with the original packaging [...] What we didn't get was the passion this very loyal small group of consumers have. That wasn't something that came out in the research," says Campbell in a telephone interview with the *New York Times*. [7]

What this story shows again is that what customers say in research can't always be trusted (we've seen that too many times in this book) and customers can feel an emotional bond even with the appearance of the product and the visual clues (brand people call it "visual equity"). There is more to it, however.

When you look into the subsequent analysis from packaging and branding professionals of why it failed, they would say it's because it parted ways with the most recognizable visual cues of the old design, that is, the name and logo "Tropicana" was turned from horizontal to vertical. The orange with the straw disappeared and was replaced with a glass of orange juice and the other changes that related to the text and flavor descriptors (i.e., no pulp, etc.) meant that consumers were confused if this is the same product that they've always loved.

I believe that there are some behavioral science heuristics in play here as well. First, just like in the "New Coke" case, I think loss aversion affects people's perceptions. People hate losing much more than they like winning. So with any change, you'd expect a bit of that. Then there is the mere-exposure (or familiarity) effect, which states that people tend to favor things they are familiar with or have been exposed to (even without them consciously recalling it). In a famous experiment, social psychologist Robert Zajonc showed people meaningless Chinese characters and told them that these symbols represented adjectives. Later people were asked if they remembered what the symbols meant but they couldn't recall any of them. Interestingly, however, when asked to rate whether the symbols held positive or negative connotations, the symbols that had been previously seen by the test subjects were consistently rated more positively than those unseen. [8]

Therefore, you'd expect to see some complaints and an initial slight drop in sales but nowhere near as dramatic as in the case of Tropicana. In addition, what you lose from parting with some old stuff you'd expect to gain a lot more from a more persuasive and emotionally appealing design that would attract new customers. Scott Young and Vincenzo Ciummo from Perception Research Services, a company that conducts over 700 consumer research studies annually to help organizations with packaging, say that they've "actually found an almost perfect bell curve, in which roughly 50 percent of proposed packaging systems outperform current packaging." [9]

They advise that in order to avoid such mistakes as in the Tropicana case, one has to start the research in the actual environment, that is, at the shelf. Understand the customer's mindset. What are customers looking for, what are the visual clues they use to recognize brands and products? Their article "Managing Risk in a Package Redesign: What Can We Learn From Tropicana?" dates from 2009 and doesn't talk about facial emotion recognition and eye-tracking technology but these are some very handy tools nowadays that help understand what customers see and how they feel at the shelves. Another interesting tip from them is asking customers to draw the packaging from memory to uncover the brand's "visual equities." It turns out there is a lot of science in package design just like there is a lot of science in customer experience and research.

People's actual behavior is highly susceptible to context. Traditional conjoint analysis is entirely removed from any decision environment a customer would ever encounter in practice, so the resultant data is distorted. So instead of the typical conjoint exercises to understand what features customers prefer the most, organizations could move to a "behavioral conjoint" where customers are presented with whole product offerings as in the real world and asked which one they'd buy. In this way, organizations could vary aspects of the product offering, language, and behavioral science nudges used in the description, to see which offering package would have the biggest impact on customer behavior. Then do some small real-life testing.

Therefore doing a more advanced form of research that takes into account that customers are not aware of their inner drivers can do wonders for you and save you from costly mistakes but even doing so and using some of the methodologies we mentioned (i.e., SEM), you may still miss 50 percent of the picture (i.e., what affects customer behavior and drives value for the organization), if you don't include emotions in your research.

In the next chapter, we will discuss how organizations can measure emotions in the offline and online world.

Practitioner Tips From This Chapter

- Take into account that customers will only tell you what is on the top of their mind (i.e., the rational aspects) and what's on the top of their mind is not necessarily what is really driving their behavior.
- Use more advanced customer research analysis techniques such as SEM, behavioral conjoint, or techniques that directly measure neurological or biological reactions (facial expressions, sweat, heart rate, electrical activity in certain areas of the brain, etc.). We'll talk more about the latter in the next chapter.

CHAPTER 7

Practice 3

Include Emotions in Your Research

The range of what we think and do is limited by what we fail to notice. And because we fail to notice that we fail to notice, there is little we can do to change; until we notice how failing to notice shapes our thoughts and deeds.

—R.D. Laing

The ASCI says that "the analytics employed to turn data into information are for the most part not good enough." I would go a step further. Even if the analytics deployed were the most advanced, if there was no data about customer emotions, the organization could still miss the biggest drivers of value in the experience.

In Chapter 2 and Table 2.5, we shared that in our research we have found that emotions affect 48 and 49 percent of value in the B2B and B2C sectors, respectively. If you recall Figure 2.1, in the middle, that is, "response", sit the emotions. So when we do our statistical analysis using SEM, we build a model where the various aspects of a company's experience, grouped in touchpoints, are linked to emotions and the value indicators (likelihood to recommend, likelihood to renew, etc.). Emotions are also linked to the value indicators. When we do the modeling, the model does a path analysis and tests the statistical significance of those links. So the aspects of the experience could have a direct effect on business value, an indirect effect on value (i.e., affecting value through emotions), or both. This way we found that the direct effects accounted for 52 and 51 percent of business value for B2B and B2C, respectively, while emotions accounted for the remainder.

This means, if you don't include emotions in your research, you could miss almost 50 percent of the picture and arrive at different conclusions and resource allocations. Yet, very few organizations measure them or include them in their research methodologies let alone have targets around them.

However, when we ask organizations "Do you measure emotions?" more often than not we hear them say "Yes." When we ask them, "How do you measure them?" we start hearing all sorts of answers that have very little to do with actual emotions. Most commonly they'll say "we ask the NPS question and also get customer comments." When we ask if they measure specific emotions such as trust, valued, cared for, and so on, almost always the answer is "no." There are of course some advanced organizations that do measure emotions and are leading the way with the latest technology advancements (AI in particular).

In Figure 1.1, we showed you the 20 emotions that we have been measuring with organizations when doing quantitative research. In addition to these we would also include other emotional aspects, more specific to the particular organization and interactions such as "support staff are empathetic to my situation," "I feel like I have a relationship with my sales representative," "the organization treats me as a valued business partner," or some more emotional motivators such as "feeling of prestige."

It's important to note that the emotions and the emotional motivators that drive customer behavior at the beginning of the sales funnel, at the conversion point, and at the retention stage might be different. For example, inspiration and curiosity might be key drivers early in the sales funnel, trust might be key at conversion, and the feelings of being cared for or being valued as a business partner are typically drivers of retention. The extent to which customers feel the different emotions could also change with the longevity of the relationship. Working with a credit card company, we created emotional profiles for new customers, customers who have been using the cards for a while, customers at the point of renewal, customers who are having financial difficulties, and those ending the relationship. It was fascinating to see how the emotional profiles change. It started with high positive emotions and low negative emotions for new customers. Then one could see how the positive emotions get lower (i.e., are felt to a smaller extent) and the negative emotions get higher (i.e., felt to a larger extent) for customers who have been with the company for a while. And when you get to those ending the relationship and with financial difficulties, it's completely reversed—the negative emotions are much higher than the positive emotions.

Given all the things we said about people, the fact that more often than not they are unaware of what truly drives their behavior, that emotions drive people's behavior mostly on an unconscious basis, and that, in general, people have a limited emotional vocabulary and find it difficult to talk about their emotions, one might be tempted to question how suitable it is to ask people about how they feel but that's an approach backed by academia. Just like when you want to ask someone how they feel you ask them, psychologists have relied on self-reports to find out how people feel, and for good reason, professor Lisa Feldman Barrett of the Northeastern University says. She received a National Institutes of Health Director's Pioneer Award for her groundbreaking research on emotion in the brain and is an elected member of the Royal Society of Canada. She says that "Decades of behavioral, cognitive, and psychophysiological research have failed to provide clear and consistent measures that unambiguously correspond to the categories of experienced emotion that are found in Western cultures." And so "If we want to know whether people feel these emotions, we have to ask them," she adds. [1]

Professor Barrett has also conducted studies on the relationship between momentary emotion experiences (i.e., how we feel when having an experience) and the retrospective ratings of emotion (i.e., how we rate those experiences several months later when asked to complete a survey). She conducted a study where participants were asked to complete an emotion measure every morning (7 a.m.–12 p.m.), afternoon (12 p.m.–5 p.m.), and evening (5 p.m.–12 a.m.) of each day for 90 consecutive days. Finally, after the 90 days were over, they completed a retrospective emotion assessment. The study concluded that "recall-based ratings of emotion contain accurate information about momentary emotion experiences." They found that the average ratings of the positive emotions across the study were a strong predictor of how respondents rated their feelings "over the past three months in general." The second strong predictor of the positive emotions category was taking the average ratings of how participants felt in the final week of the study. When it comes to the negative emotions, the strongest predictors were how respondents felt at the peak of the negative emotions and the average across the study. The main conclusion was that "the momentary ratings of emotion were strongly related to the retrospective ratings, regardless of the summary index chosen." [2] What I also found interesting in these findings was that apparently, retrospective ratings of emotions (i.e., asking customers to rate the extent they feel certain emotions in their experience with you as an organization) are inclusive of the peak–end rule, that is, how customers have felt at the peak of their experience (according to professor Barrett's study, only as far as the negative peak is concerned) and at the end of the experience (although only as far as the positive emotions are concerned). Therefore our advice to organizations is not to be shy about asking customers about how they feel and to measure customer emotions.

When it comes to digital experiences and digital content there is also a set of tools that are very handy at evaluating the experience and the triggers of customer behavior. Facial expressions analysis (facial emotion recognition) is one of those as it allows you to authentically measure what emotions customers feel as they are having a digital experience. Our face is a gateway to how we feel. The moment your wife walks into the room you can tell by the look on her face whether she feels joyful or angry about something. I find it funny and heartbreaking at the same time when the face of my little son changes to a sad grimace almost to the point of crying when we deny him a request or when we tell him off about something. We can "read" into how people feel based on changes in key facial features. While we are hardwired from birth to express and read emotion (neither your mother nor your teacher told you what face to put when you are happy or told you how to read other people's faces), achieving this task with a computer algorithm took some time to figure out (efforts date back to at least the 1970s). Recent advancements in computer vision and ML, however, made it possible to detect emotion from images and videos. Emotion recognition is based on the analysis of key facial landmark positions (e.g., end of nose, eyebrows, lips, cheeks). It relies on coding of the actions of individual or groups of muscles typically seen when producing the facial expressions of a particular emotion. Depending on the algorithm, facial expressions can be classified into seven basic emotions (e.g., joy/happiness, confusion/anger, fear, disgust, contempt, sadness, and surprise). Those "basic" emotions can be traced back to Darwin but, in the context we are talking about, they were put in the spotlight in the 1970s by Paul Ekman, an emeritus research psychologist at UC Berkeley and one of the early pioneers in the field of emotions and their relation to facial expressions. Better trained algorithms can also recognize additional emotions such as confusion, frustration, the nonexpression of emotion, and compound emotions (e.g., happily surprised, happily disgusted, sadly surprised, sadly angry). In addition, some algorithms don't just rely on facial expressions but also can infer emotion by analyzing the hue of people's faces. You know how people's faces turn red from anger or when they are embarrassed (it's probably most visible on white people's faces). It's caused by changes in the diameter of blood vessels in our body and in the face in particular, which allow more blood to flow into the muscles. Apparently, these facial blood flow changes match up to the type of expression and some algorithms can detect the type of emotion and its valence on another person's face even if their facial expression doesn't change. [3]

We started to look into incorporating facial emotion recognition into our toolset after I made a trip to China where I was challenged by a bank executive who was skeptical about asking people how they feel. We tested the technology with a timeshare website. We found that most of the time during our experience using the website, there were no emotions felt, but the most predominantly felt emotions were "sad" and "disgusted." Not what you'd want in a holiday booking experience. The website was too cluttered with many and sometimes confusing options and so on. It was quite powerful to see the emotions as it's not just an opinion anymore but there is data about how customers have actually felt.

To gain better and more actionable insights, organizations can supplement facial emotion recognition data with eye-tracking data. Eye-tracking data can deliver valuable insights into the gaze patterns of your website visitors, for example:

- How long does it take website visitors to find a specific product on your site?
- Which kind of visual information do they ignore (but are supposed to respond to)?

- Where do your website visitors look? What do they look at and how much time do they spend looking at it?
- What is the order in which visual elements are fixated upon?
- Does an individual's gaze return to a visual element that was looked at before?

In combination with the eye-tracking and facial recognition toolset, you could also add a smartwatch-looking wrist device that measures the galvanic skin response (GSR). GSR measures changes in electrical (ionic) activity resulting from changes in sweat gland activity. These are reflective of the intensity of our emotional state/arousal (positive or negative). Facial expressions can be voluntary or involuntary (fake or genuine) and a certain percentage of people don't express anything but they still feel, so the combination with GSR allows you to distinguish the genuine emotions and their intensity. This is very important when you consider Kahneman's peak–end rule (i.e., we don't choose between experiences but between the memories of the experiences and what people remember are the peak moments and the endings). The GSR can help you find the emotional peaks in the experience.

Facial emotion recognition can of course be used not just to assess digital experiences. Advertisers can measure unfiltered and unbiased consumer emotional responses to digital content. The technology can also be used to analyze customer emotions to gauge their reaction to goods or their arrangement within the shop, pharmacy, and so on. Walmart, for example, has made a patent filing, as reported by USA Today, for a system that envisions using video to scan for customers who are frustrated or unhappy so help can be dispatched. [4] Getting extra help to a shopper without one having to ask for it is a nice personal touch. This will also give Walmart real-time customer experience data allowing managers to take action and address customer service issues. This would improve return visits and reduce social media gripes. Walmart isn't explicit about what they will use the system for and haven't commented on the topic, but knowing the technology's capabilities we could also guess that it'll allow them to also know which products customers like the most (so they know when they have a hot product in hand and can display it more prominently), how music influences shoppers' mood at different times of the day, and much more. My favorite and most creative application of the technology though, so far, comes from Teatreneu, a popular comedy club in Barcelona, Spain. Facing a declining audience the club decided not to charge for admission but to charge each customer 30 euro cents for every laugh during a performance, up to a limit of €24 (US$28.47). Facial recognition technology was fixed to the back of the seats to capture the reactions. No laughs, no pay. In the end, overall ticket prices increased by €6 (US$7.12), and attendance rose 35 percent. [5]

We need to put a couple of notes of caution when it comes to facial emotion recognition as we know people have a soft spot for shiny new technologies. For once, the technology has been found to be less accurate on certain ethnicities, although that may be less of a problem in a year or two as the algorithm is improving the more data is fed to it. In the public domain, this technology is always associated with privacy concerns but those stem mostly from the use of the technology by government surveillance units, using AI algorithms, which are no less prone to biases than the people who taught them how to analyze data, to shift through CVs, and so on. For the purposes that we've talked about, that's not so much of an issue because if it's used as part of a study, people are free to participate (and are mostly remunerated for it) just like they are free to take a survey or not. It's done either by sitting at their home and using their laptop, phone, or tablet camera or in a lab setting. Then, if we talk about using the technology in a shop, the data is anonymized (the camera doesn't know your name anyway), encrypted, mostly it gets destroyed within a day or a week, and all the results are analyzed and aggregated by the AI. On top of that, experts say that we share abnormally more personal data and sensitive data by using a public wifi network but no one complains about public wifis.

The second note of caution regarding facial emotion measurement is that it doesn't capture more inner and deeper emotions such as trust, cared for, valued, appreciated, and respected. As you know, sometimes it takes time and multiple interactions for those to be formed. Our research also showed that those are key value-driving emotions. I always felt that those are key omissions and as I did the research for this chapter I was glad to find that professor Barrett shares the same opinion. And she's found scientific evidence to back it up. She is not a big fan of the "basic" emotions as "research led her to realize that one can experience specific emotions without having characteristic facial expressions." [6] As we've shared earlier, her advice if you want to know how people feel is to ask them.

Facial emotion recognition technology can be very useful to measure a customer's instinctive and authentic reaction when having an interaction with a product, when having a digital experience, when viewing an advertisement, or staring at the shelves. At the same time, organizations can use survey mechanisms to measure emotions, find what stimulates those emotions, and ultimately, where they should focus their efforts to drive customer retention, engagement, and so on.

You can also get to customer emotions with customer interviews and focus groups. The important thing here is to treat the process as "peeling an onion." You need to dig deeper and read between the lines to get to the root-cause drivers of customer behavior. Here we should also mention a piece of advice from Aarron Walter, the founder of the UX practice in MailChimp and author of *Designing for Emotion*, whom we've talked about in Chapter 5. In this agile world, quite often business product owners, UX designers, and programmers will be pushing to get the product market-ready and when the issue of emotional design is brought up they'll say "we can add it later." Consider this though, 77 percent of users never use an app again 72 hours after installing. [7] So emotional design shouldn't be an afterthought. Whether it's by spending time talking and observing customers using qualitative empathy maps or doing some more advanced and sophisticated research using SEM or facial emotion recognition technology, it's important to base your new product, service, or experience design on insights that take customer emotions into account.

The key thing to remember from this chapter is to include customer emotions in your research or else you may miss 50 percent of the big picture and focus on deceiving aspects or things that may not give you as much return.

Now that we have discussed how important emotions are and how to go about doing research on the key emotions in your customer experience, in the next chapter, we will share how leading organizations are not leaving their experience to chance. We'll talk about what they do to equip their staff with the skills to evoke the targeted emotions and how a study in two luxury clothing retailers in California revealed that trust can be reciprocal and when the sales associates' brains release more oxytocin it makes customers more likely to purchase.

Practitioner Tips From This Chapter

- Include emotions in your quantitative and qualitative research. You can start by measuring some of the emotions as in our pyramid of emotions (Figure 1.1) or some of the attributes of emotional attachment that you find most relevant in your experience (Table 2.3). Then, find which of these emotions drive the most value for your organization at the different stages of the customer journey.
- You can also measure emotions authentically, without relying on customers self-rating, the extent to which they feel certain emotions by using techniques that directly measure neurological and biological reactions (e.g., facial emotion recognition, GSR, eye tracking).

CHAPTER 8

Practice 4

Be Deliberate About the Emotions You Want to Evoke and How to Evoke Them

People will forget what you said, people will forget what you did, but people will never forget how you made them feel

—Maya Angelou

We spoke in the previous chapters about how important emotions are in the customer experience and how to include them in your research. Now let us ask you this. What emotions do you want to evoke in your customers? Is there a consensus within the organization? Are people aware of those and do they know how to go about evoking those emotions?

Go around the organization and ask the question "What is the experience our organization is trying to deliver?" Ask executives or managers in meetings to write down their answers on post-it notes. Surely this wouldn't be a hard exercise. It's a simple enough question, right? And yet, chances are that most people will gaze at you as if they want to ask you: "Is this a trick question?" or "Are you trying to trick me?" Still, when people write what they think is the experience your organization is trying to deliver, most likely you'd see things like "deliver a world-class experience," "best industry experience," "quality customer service," "be efficient and fast," "reliable," "transparent," and "wow customers."

We have found this simple question to be very insightful and game-changing. Naturally, people will aspire to a vision of a good customer experience but they all have slightly different visions. Some will want to be fast, others would bet on reliability, some might be thinking "wow"-ing customers is what would make them buy more, some might want to stay within their roots and be "traditional," while others might be thinking you should be "innovative" and "modern." These are all nice things (other than "wow"-ing customers; we don't believe it's a sustainable and achievable strategy to wow all customers all the time...) but you can see that they are also conflicting things. Thus different departments might be working according to their own vision and pulling the organization in different directions when it comes to customer experience.

Therefore, organizations need to define the experience they are trying to deliver. They can use it as a "north star" to ensure the organization is aligned around that common understanding and moving in the same direction. A key part of that definition should be about what emotions you want your customers to feel in the experience. This would also make the job of the customer experience manager easier as she can go to people and say "hey, we've agreed that we want customers to feel X, what you are doing goes against that feeling."

So it is about being deliberate in evoking the key emotions in your experience. Ideally, before you do that, you'd have done some research to indeed find which emotions are the key drivers of value for the organization.

Earlier in the book, in Chapter 3, we've mentioned a U.S.-based global logistics company that found emotions to be contributing to 46 percent of the brand attachment and share of wallet. So they came to us and with the help of professor Ryan Hamilton and his team, we created a training course manual for their contact center team to equip them with the knowledge and skills on how to evoke their key emotions. We looked at the psychology of why those emotions are important, the moments when we feel these emotions, how to evoke those emotions, and the signs that customers are indeed feeling these emotions or feel the opposite.

The organization has been measuring these emotions for a while and since the implementation of the manual and training, they reported that the top box scores for most of those emotions had improved by 10 percent, while the top box score for the question "If you had your own company focused on customer service, would you hire the agent you spoke to" had increased by staggering 25 percent.

Another organization that we've helped create their Customer Experience Statement was Maersk Line. At the time, they were looking to differentiate and move away from competing on the spiraling down shipping rates. They recognized that they had a well-known brand and they wanted to make it a premium brand. With a premium brand, you also need a premium service. So, in order to move away from the feeling of just being another transaction and create a feeling of a relationship, they chose to focus on three emotions: *trust, cared for,* and *valued.* Those were also emotions that our research had identified as key drivers of value. This, along with the rest of the activities in their transformational customer experience program, led to an increase in their Net Promoter Score® (NPS) from −10 to +40 percentage points in 30 months. The smart people working in their offices managed to calculate that for each 4 percentage point improvement in their NPS, cargo volume increased by 1 percent. [1] We know that in the shipping industry, most of the time, operations managers will be asking for quotes from several different companies and relying on Request for Proposal (RFP), but when there is the need for an urgent or ad hoc shipment they can shift volume to whichever carrier they feel most comfortable working with. Thus with improving the customer experience Maersk Line also increased the cargo volume shipped with them.

When we did our database research subject of this book, we found Emotional attachment to be the biggest driver of value. Then, I thought, well, if Emotional attachment is the biggest driver of value, which of the traditional touchpoints drive Emotional attachment.

So I reanalyzed the models where Emotional attachment was the biggest driver of value (i.e., in 35 out of the 59 models) and found that, across the various industries, Customer service (here we mean mostly call center interactions) has the biggest effect on Emotional attachment with 21 percent. Next comes Brand & advertising with 19 percent, followed by Product & use and Communications both with 15 percent contribution toward Emotional attachment (see Table 8.1).

It is therefore really important to be deliberate and equip your customer-facing employees with the soft skills needed to evoke the key value-driving emotions.

Starbucks is one of those companies that don't leave their experience to the chance that their new recruits know how to handle customers and deliver their desired experience. In their "Green Apron Book," freshmen get information on how to get involved in the company; on crafted

Table 8.1 *What drives Emotional attachment?*

	Effect on Emotional attachment (%)
Customer service	21
Brand & advertising	19
Product & use	15
Communications	15
Buy	9
Retain	6
Learn	6
Get onboard	4
Billing & payment	3
Web & self-service	0

language, modeled behaviors, efficiency on the floor; on the psychology of customer expectations; and on mantras to follow.

Apple is probably the most sophisticated company out there when it comes to training frontline staff. New recruits at their stores are trained over three weeks following the "Genius Training Manual." Employees go through courses for psychological mastery, learn about banned words, and, using role-playing exercises, learn how to empathize with customers, console them, cheer them up, and correct various Genius Bar confrontations. Apple wouldn't be Apple if, of course, employees didn't go through a module on how to identify and capitalize on human emotions by judging body language to make the sale.

As Apple's training manual suggests, targeting specific emotions is not just a practice for the customer service staff but also for sales associates. A LinkedIn report titled "Rethink the B2B buyer's journey," [2] for example, lists "trust" and "personal relationships" as the top two reasons for vendor relationships getting stronger, with 52 and 48 percent of respondents mentioning them respectively.

Trust is an interesting and important emotion in sales. A study by Paul J. Zak, [3] a professor of economics, psychology, and management at Claremont Graduate University and author of *Trust Factor: The Science of Creating High-Performance Companies* found that trust directly drives sales. He and his team conducted research in two luxury clothing stores in California where staff wore sensors that measure the physiologic effects of oxytocin release in the brain.

Oxytocin is a hormone and a neurotransmitter that has physical and psychological effects, including influencing social behavior and emotion. Academic research shows that brain oxytocin modulates social behaviors, including maternal care and aggression, pair bonding, sexual behavior, social memory, support, and human trust, and downregulates stress responses, including anxiety. [4] It is oxytocin that allows us to feel empathy, that is, to understand and share the emotions of others.

Research also suggests that oxytocin release can be reciprocal—if our interaction causes your brain to make oxytocin, it will typically do the same for mine. This made Paul Zak and his team hypothesize that oxytocin release in salespeople would predict increased trust in customers (customers were not asked to wear sensors so that they had a natural shopping experience uninterrupted by the experiment).

They were right! Using an index of neural measures which they call "immersion" (measuring attention and oxytocin release), they found that the index predicted with 69 percent accuracy who made a purchase. They also found that the amount a customer spent increased linearly with immersion.

In practice, what the sales associates were doing at peak immersion was to share product narratives, offer personalized recommendations for products, and provide some unexpected, "above and beyond" experiences, such as offering refreshments or carrying a customer's shopping bag. As you can see, each of these aspects that create an immersive selling ceremony can be taught and learned with practice.

All our research and experience working with organizations suggests that human-to-human interactions are great drivers of emotions (one way or another), so don't leave those to chance. Be deliberate and equip your employees with the skills needed to be masters of these interactions.

An organization can be deliberate about evoking certain emotions not just through human-to-human interactions. TUI Travel is a company that springs to my mind when I think about a carefully designed omnichannel experience focused around some specific emotions. TUI Travel is a British leisure travel group, which at the time was operating separately from its German parent TUI Group—the largest leisure travel and tourism company in the world, owning airlines, travel agent companies, hotels, resorts, and so on. Many years ago I turned to our database with the questions—"Which companies rank the highest on specific positive emotions" and "What do they do to evoke them that other companies can learn from?" When I looked at our benchmarking data, I found that TUI Travel PLC ranked the highest on some specific emotions, that is, happy, pleased, and safe. At the same time, they also ranked the lowest on making their customers feel "hurried." Now, for a leisure company that sends its customers to lie on a sunbed near the beach and drink cocktails, ranking the highest on feeling happy and pleased was not really that surprising for me (although anyone who had spent time working in the tourism industry will tell you that tourists are the most demanding and with most absurd complaints). What really intrigued me is that for a company whose business is centered around sending British tourists to places like Egypt and Morocco, they had scored the highest on "Safe." "Hurried" was also an outlier for me, considering all the hassle about being on time for all the flights, shuttle busses, bus tours, and so on. At the time I did research, we were working with a subsidiary of British Airways so when I shared the insights with the client team, one of the team members jumped up. She said that the insights really resonate with her because she had just used them for her vacation. So she sent me some of the communications that were sent to her. The company had designed a carefully thought communication campaign. They mix in the communication e-mail things that would get the customer excited with things that would evoke the feeling of safety and also include some upsell messages. So, for example, safety aspects will be prominently featured right in the first e-mail customers receive after booking. "Remember, we keep your ticket safe for you in your portal area," the customer reads. Then further down the customer sees a "Health and Safety" icon in the side area of the e-mail, just underneath the "Getting to the Airport" and "Passports, Visas and Baggage" icons. The common theme in those early communications is "just bring your passports." Then, in their fifth e-mail, which comes with the subject line "your last-minute checklist," they show a calendar with a two-day countdown, they show a seven-day weather forecast to get the customer excited, and, toward the end of the e-mail, at a specially shaded area, they provide the contact details for the British Embassy in the country. Regarding the feeling of "unhurried," they also say in that e-mail "it's not too late to log in" and do things like "check your hotel video," "print your itinerary," "get directions to the airport." As we've said many times, a good customer experience is also one that sells more and among those last-minute options is "plan where to visit on your holiday." Those emotions are reinforced along the transit and during the holiday experience. Checking in and boarding are specially thought-through so that it's all done in an orderly fashion and families can sit in and relax. The safety messages are very prominent throughout the journey. Upon arriving in the hotel, it all starts with a safety briefing. When you talk to company executives you understand that this is a real strategy because even "the representatives portray maturity as they are not the 18-year-olds so typical of the industry," they say. Then on top of that, the organization provides Text and Mobile service, a 24/7 phone line, and should anything happen, they will send someone for support, find a doctor, and help with the paperwork. The continuous enforcement of their high standards for the intended experience is made possible by their relentless push for feedback from customers. Upon return, all customers are asked to provide feedback. That's not just a measurement and tracking mechanism but also one geared toward insights and the next sale. The goal is not just to get a rating for the various hotels and employees but also to hear customers' stories and understand the drivers behind the different types of travelers (i.e., what are the peak moments for different customers, etc.). The ask for feedback is another selling opportunity as well. There is a "where next" section with a social proof-type nudge, that is, "people who have enjoyed X country also enjoy Y and Z."

This is just one example of how an organization can target certain emotions in the online and offline experience. The main thing here is that the organization had a purposeful design from the booking confirmation until after the customer has returned from her holiday. None of the things we mentioned were a stand-out by itself but this is the thing with emotions; oftentimes it's the little things throughout the journey that add up. More often than not, these things go by without us noticing them just as the person from our client's team, who had just returned from holiday, had not paid much attention to these little clues until we brought up the subject. Then it all bubbled up just like most customers will have a feel whether they like a company or not but would have a hard time explaining the real reasons why they like it. When asked though, their "Interpreter Brain" will cite the first two to three big things that come to mind because those are the ones that would make most logical sense. However, when it comes to customer experience it's often the little thoughtful things along the journey that create the feeling of an attachment toward an organization. Think about the hotel chains and airlines you like the most. Chances are that they are not doing anything different from other comparable businesses but they do a number of small things right consistently. If you put your management hat on, you'd see that, in order for them to do those things, they must have the right recruitment, training, coaching, measurement, and systems to catch customer data and preferences (not to mention thoughtful customer and employee engagement strategies). This is what makes a deliberate experience. Most organizations, however, will lack this kind of coherent strategy based around a common vision about the experience the organization wants to deliver and the emotions the organization is trying to evoke.

As we've said, the aforementioned is not confined to face-to-face interactions only. Nowadays companies are also trying to make the AI-powered customer interactions feel more human-like by giving the AI a face (that of a human or of an animal mascot), breaking the experience and tasks into small chunks, using more jargon, and so on.

The key is to be deliberate about the emotions you want to evoke and how to evoke them, whether in digital or employee interactions. Employees' payroll may appear as a big cost item on the balance sheet but as our research and experience shows in many instances it could be a key value-driving factor.

Performance, though, is a function of ability times motivation. Defining the experience you want to deliver that is based around the key value drivers in the experience and equipping employees with the skills and knowledge to deliver the desired experience addresses the ability part of that performance equation. But what about employee motivation? Are your employees engaged enough to be your brand ambassadors? And, if emotions are key to personal and business relationships, are they the key for employee engagement too? We will look into that in the next chapter.

Practitioner Tips From This Chapter

- Map the customer journey and decide what key emotions you'd want customers to feel at certain moments of the journey. Ideally, those will be emotions that your research with customers shows that would drive value for the organization.
- Design the experience to trigger these emotions.
- Develop a training course and train the management and customer-facing teams (managers so they could provide coaching and drive the metrics; customer-facing employees so they are equipped with the skills to master the interaction and evoke the desired emotions).
- Measure these emotions with customers.

CHAPTER 9

Practice 5

Aim for the Same Emotions in the Employee Experience

People's tendency is to overestimate how visible their emotions are to others.
—Kerry R. Gibson, Kate O'Leary, Joseph R. Weintraub

Imagine this scenario: Ben works in a large multinational organization. Last night he worked very late to deliver on a project but he still feels obliged to turn up for work at 8 a.m. just like any other day and he certainly hasn't heard to do otherwise from his manager... not today, not ever....

He has been working there for a number of years but all that has earned him was a card at his desk with a post-it note to mark his anniversary at the company. He hardly ever gets praise, recognition, or a personal word from his manager. He also feels the organization isn't sharing the gains from the recent growth with him as his salary has barely changed for years, despite the rising cost of living. It's not so hard to relate to Ben's imaginative story, is it? Because that's the reality for many employees.

In the previous chapters, we shared evidence that emotions are key to personal and business relationships. Are they the key to employee engagement too?

A 2014 American Psychological Association survey about work and well-being found that only about half of U.S. workers feel their employers are open and upfront with them and one-quarter of Americans say they simply don't trust the companies they work for. [1] This is a big deal because another research from professor Paul J. Zak shows that compared with people at low-trust companies, people at high-trust companies report:

- 74 percent less stress
- 106 percent more energy at work
- 50 percent higher productivity
- 13 percent fewer sick days
- 76 percent more engagement
- 29 percent more satisfaction with their lives
- 40 percent less burnout [2]

While this relies on self-reported scores, interestingly, Paul and his team also found that employees earn an additional $6,450 a year (17 percent more), at companies in the highest quartile of trust, compared with those in the lowest quartile. In a highly competitive labor market, this can only occur if employees at high-trust companies are more productive and innovative, they say.

Other interesting insights come from Gallup's meta-analysis of their data spanning several decades. Gallup has been doing countless employee engagement studies and has been measuring employee engagement on behalf of many Fortune 500 companies. I recall a story working with a Fortune 500 company in the Middle East that was using Gallup to measure and benchmark their employee engagement. They told us that they got one of the lowest employee engagement scores on record among all the companies Gallup has been doing studies for. Rather than addressing the real issues, employees of that company told us with a fair degree of cynicism that management held sessions explaining to them how to go about rating the questions in the survey. Needless to say, we told them to stop doing that. Gallup's meta-analysis shows that high employee engagement is linked to higher productivity, better-quality products, and increased profitability.

Gallup discovered the 12 most revealing questions [3] associated with almost all the goals a typical manager would care about: the employees' engagement, retention, productivity, and profitability—even the satisfaction of the organization's customers. Among those 12 are:

1. In the last seven days I have received recognition or praise for good work (i.e., implies a sense of belonging/feeling of a relationship).
2. My supervisor, or someone at work, seems to care about me as a person (implies caring).
3. There is someone at work who encourages my development (implies understanding, caring).
4. I have a best friend at work (implies relationship).

In their book *The Power of Moments*, Chip and Dan Heath make the observation about how similar the first three are to the questions professor Harry T. Reis (Chapter 3) pinned as predictors of personal relationships strength (i.e., *understanding*—my partner knows me; *validation*—my partner respects me; and *caring*—my partner is supportive of me). And as we've said earlier, in our research with customers, we found those emotions to be key value drivers. Employees want to feel recognition for their work, just like customers want to know that their custom over the years is appreciated and they are recognized as long-term members. This goes back to Maslow's concept of a sense of belonging as a basic human need.

Then Question 2 talks about "care for me as a person" in the employee satisfaction questionnaire. Care sits at the top of our list of most value-driving aspects that formed the Emotional attachment touchpoint (see Table 2.3). In B2B settings, when we've conducted research we have used the exact same wording—"cares about me as a person"—and that turned out to be a key value driver in many instances. Question 3 also implies caring, this time about the development of the employee, while the last question looks at whether some deep personal relationships have been formed at work.

We have conducted our Emotional Signature® research with organizations focusing on the employee experience and all that we've said in this book holds true when it comes to the employee experience as well. For example, working with a U.S. insurer, we found that one of the key value-driving aspects of the employee experience was "I feel valued as a team member." That was also a subconscious driver as employees had said they wanted a lot more of other things. We also found that emotional engagement dropped significantly with longer employee tenure, which was an alarming signal and something that is the opposite of what is happening in most organizations (normally employees 20 to 39 are less engaged as they are not so involved in decision making and earn less, while the opposite is typically true for more senior employees).

What Drives Employee Engagement?

In a report for the Institute of Employment Studies, researchers Gemma Robertson-Smith and Carl Markwick make a comprehensive literature review of the studies on employee engagement. They find that there is no silver bullet when it comes to it but nevertheless some key aspects emerge more frequently than others. In their report, they cite a study by The Conference Board, which found that 26 different drivers of engagement were proposed in 12 largely consultancy-based studies of employee engagement. The most commonly reported drivers were trust and integrity, the nature of the job, the line of sight between individual performance and company performance, career growth opportunities, pride in the company, relationships with coworkers/team members, employee development, and the personal relationship with one's manager. [4] We'll talk about some of these things and what can organizations do about them but before we do that, when you read the report, we couldn't help noticing some key emotions reappearing throughout the report. The emotion "trust" is mentioned 21 times, respect is mentioned 12 times, and, while feeling appreciated is mentioned just once, recognition is mentioned 10 times which for us is closely related to the feeling of appreciation. We will look into those key for employee engagement emotions in the next paragraphs.

How to Create a Feeling of *Trust* in Employees?

In his HBR article "The Neuroscience of Trust," professor Paul J. Zak, who we've mentioned multiple times in this book, recommends recognizing excellence. I'd say that recognizing people in front of their peers is also a form of social proof that encourages others to follow the example set by others and provides guidelines into what is culturally accepted and promoted in the workplace.

Then, it's important that teams are assigned difficult but achievable tasks. Difficult so they feel stimulated and energized but also achievable so they don't give up before they've even begun. Managers should check in the progress and adjust goals that are out of reach. I have learned that when some goals are important to senior managers they would check often on your progress. At the same time when they sometimes give you an ambitious or nebulous task with an unclear link to company priorities and then never check on you, you quickly learn that is something you can drop from your list of to-do things and no one would even notice.

Giving people space for discretion and greater control of how they work is also a mutual trust-building factor. In the employee engagement study we did with a U.S. insurer, an attribute we tested was "I feel I can be my true self at work." Employees rated it the lowest in terms of importance of all 40 aspects we tested and yet it was one of the biggest drivers of employee engagement and ambassadorship (i.e., employee commitment, belief in the vision and purpose of the organization, and likelihood to promote it to others). For employee ambassadorship, it is also very important that the senior management often communicate the company's vision and strategic objectives.

Finally, it's noteworthy to say that you can be intentional about building relationships at the workplace. As The Conference Board study and numerous other studies have shown, the personal relationship with one's manager is key to employee engagement and those are also the people who can most easily and most often provide recognition for employees' work. Paul J. Zak shares evidence about this in his HBR article "The Neuroscience of Trust." He cites a Google study which found that managers who "express interest in and concern for team members' success and personal well-being" outperform others in the quality and quantity of their work while another study of software engineers in Silicon Valley found that those who connected with others and helped them with their projects not only earned the respect and trust of their peers but were also more productive themselves. So managers can make it a habit to spend time walking around the organization and meeting with their subordinates and peers, organizing social events that foster the creation of personal relationships (remember one of Gallup's key 12 questions was "I have a best friend at work"), and so on.

Asking for help may also help in this regard. This way a manager can show appreciation for one's skills and strengths. There may be a deeper psychological effect too. I think there may be something of the Benjamin Franklin effect too. When Benjamin Franklin, born one of 17 children to poor parents, came for re-election as a civil clerk, his opponent delivered a long speech aiming to harm his reputation. Although the future Founding Father won the election, he was rather concerned about future frictions with this gentleman of "fortune and education," he writes in his autobiography. So Franklin wanted to turn this adversary into an ally but without paying too much respect to him. Having heard that he had in his library a "very scarce and curious book," Franklin writes him a courteous letter requesting to borrow the book. After a week, he returned the book with a note expressing his gratitude for the favor. The next time they met, this former adversary spoke to him with "great civility" (which he had never done before) and manifested readiness to serve him on all occasions, Franklin writes. From that day on, they became friends for the rest of their lives. "He that has once done you a kindness will be more ready to do you another, than he whom you yourself have obliged." [5] This became known as the Benjamin Franklin effect. People reason that they help others because they like them, even if they do not because their minds are in a state of cognitive dissonance and struggle to maintain logical consistency between their actions and perceptions. In our case though, with managers asking for help, it is not so much that their subordinates and peers are their adversaries (although it shouldn't be ruled out that some may have their antipathies) but the fact that once people have given someone a favor or a helpful hand they may be more likely to do it again in future and feel a closer connection with that person.

How to Create a Feeling of *Respect* in Employees?

In *Chapter 5* we spoke about the psychology of feeling respect and that respect from the group shapes social engagement, self-esteem, and health. People in managerial and high-status roles tend to feel respected on a more regular basis and thus may underestimate it as an issue that needs deliberate attention in the workplace. What we do and how we feel at work are central to how we perceive ourselves, so the lack of respect could be very detrimental. This is especially true for the younger workforce who develop themselves as people and professionals in their workplace environment. Diversity and inclusion are key trends for organizations now and not allowing discrimination is a great place to start forging a culture of respect in the workplace. Among the things that create the feeling of respect are showing empathy, compassion, sharing one's own feelings to enable the building of connections, using words of understanding to show you see other people's perspective, fostering a culture of collaboration and cooperation, but above all, words of encouragement and appreciation. Respecting employees' time during work and off-work hours can also go a long way particularly at times when many people work from home. The case of a woman who quit her job after being called into the office for a six-minute meeting was widely reported. Portia Twidt reported having to dress up, drop her children at day care, and drive to the office for a face-to-face meeting, but when it turned out that all that was for a six-minute meeting she decided to call it a day and quit her job as a research compliance specialist. [6] So scheduling unnecessary meetings is one of those things that show a lack of respect and that's something that many people and organizations are guilty of.

How to Make Employees Feel *Appreciated*?

As The Conference Board's review of research on employee engagement showed, personal relationship with one's manager is oftentimes a key driver. Adam Grant and Francesca Gino have found that a manager's expression of gratitude increases productivity. [7] Among the many experiments they did on the link between gratitude and prosocial behavior was a study with fundraisers at a public U.S. university. Students were split into two groups: gratitude and nongratitude conditions. Both groups received feedback about their effectiveness. The only difference was that after the first week of efforts to raise money, the gratitude condition group received a visit from the director of annual giving to express gratitude and appreciation of their contribution toward the university. In the week following the gratitude visit, the group that received the visit increased the number of calls they made by 51 percent. This was done purely to help the university, as fundraisers received a fixed salary and were not rewarded for effort. The researchers' conclusion was that "gratitude expressions increase prosocial behavior by enabling individuals to feel socially valued."

Many managers are, however, struggling to make employees feel that their efforts and skills are noticed and appreciated. Researchers from the Babson College of Business argue that is due to the *illusion of transparency*, that is, people's tendency to overestimate how visible their emotions are to others. [8] Talking to employees and managers, they found that there is a gap between how much managers appreciate employees and how much employees feel appreciated. They attribute that gap partly to managers incorrectly assuming that employees knew how they felt about them and partly due to having trouble expressing appreciation. As we've said multiple times in this book, emotions often work on an unconscious level so don't be surprised that it is the little things that create the feeling of appreciation. Things like dropping by to say "Hello" and "How are you," providing some coaching, and telling people they can come in late the day after working long hours or after a transatlantic flight (as has often been the case with me) can do wonders for team managers.

Emotions like trust, respect, and appreciation have been proven to be key to driving employee engagement and productivity and they should feature and be measured in employee engagement programs. Organizations, however, could also opt in for targeting the same emotions with employees as they do for customers. This way, employees can see what it means to evoke and feel these emotions. It would also be cynical for the organization to be asking employees to make customers feel certain emotions but doing the opposite for them. When we were recently presenting what the global team of a pharmaceutical company had selected as their Customer Experience Statement, the head of HR immediately spotted that they can use the same emotions in their employee experience. We were glad this didn't have to come out of our mouths. Another former client of ours, in her new company, introduced five emotions that they would target in both their customer and employee experiences. They even created a logo for the e5 as they call them.

The key takeaway is that emotions are as important for the customer experience as for the employee experience. Being deliberate about what emotions to evoke in both and equipping managers with the skills needed will be key for the success and sustainability of your customer experience program. What are the other factors and why so many programs fail to deliver results will be presented in the next chapter.

Practitioner Tips From This Chapter

- Be deliberate about the emotions you want to evoke in your employee experience.
- Emotions such as feeling trust, feeling respected, and appreciated (recognized) are proven to drive employee engagement and value for the organization.
- Senior executives have a role to communicate the higher purpose and values of the organization; create a culture based on respect, trust, and recognition.
- The personal relationship with one's manager is key to employee engagement and managers can be taught how to be intentional about building relationships at the workplace and providing recognition to employees.
- You may also opt to target the same emotions for your employees as for your customers.

CHAPTER 10

Practice 6

Make Your Customer Experience Program Sustainable

The job of CX executives is to break the ego of business unit leaders
—Michael Brown

Focusing on specific emotions in the customer and employee experience that are proven to drive value would increase the odds for a successful customer experience program and gaining exponential benefits. And that's huge because right now, the odds are that roughly two out of three customer experience programs (or we'd rather hope that they are set as functions) will fail to deliver tangible benefits. This is despite the fact that various studies have been consistently stating that the vast majority of executives believe that customer experience is the key to differentiate. Research by Engage Hub from 2018 even found that 65 percent of C-level executives rank improving customer experience as the most important overall business objective, even above net profit and revenue growth. [1]

Contrast that with the fact that a number of customer experience indexes, which measure the level of service leading companies provide, have either been stagnant for years, as is the case with Forrester's and KPMG Nunwood's indexes, or even fall behind, as is the case with the United Kingdom's Customer Satisfaction Index (UKCSI) which has peaked in 2017 and has dipped since then. Similarly, as we've shared in Chapter 6, the ASCI has been in sharp decline since 2019. In fact, they say that "as of the second quarter of 2021, almost 80 percent of the companies have now failed to increase the satisfaction of their customers since

2010." [2] Bob Thompson, the founder and editor of Customer Think, an online media outlet dedicated to customer experience, says that his study found just 23 percent of respondents claim tangible benefits from CX investments, and only 30 percent claim success in terms of tangible benefits or differentiation. [3]

Now, why is that? Clearly, customer experience has been around for a long time. As we wrote at the beginning of this book, Pine and Gilmore's 1998 book and HBR article "Welcome to the Experience Economy" set the stage for competing on experiences rather than product or service and has had a profound and ripple effect not just in boardrooms but in future CX professionals and book authors. There have been hundreds of books and hundreds of thousands of posts dedicated to customer experience since then. So it's not for the lack of drum beats or of knowledge (albeit scattered around).

I don't think it's for the lack of funding either. I'm far from saying that every customer experience manager got all the funding they wanted but clearly a lot of funds have been devoted to customer experience programs and initiatives.

So why do customer experience programs fail? Here's my take.

First of all, the CX function should be set right. It should be set as a function to drive continuous improvement (that means change) and innovation based on customer insights. But from our experience, we have seen that this is not how most programs are set. All too often we see organizations assemble a cross-functional team with the task to look at improving the customer experience. So far so good. But then the teams get disassembled after a year or so. Often the reason for that is because the organization had provided the budget on a project basis rather than on an ongoing vision for a function set to drive continuous improvement based on customer insights. This means that the learnings and the momentum from the initiative often get lost.

As we have said, there is a lot of science in customer experience. There is psychology and behavioral science, science in research and measurement, and data science, and there are also skills required to lead team innovation sessions and change. So the teams need support, training, and time to go through a learning curve. Then there is the whole aspect of implementation. It can take a while for the innovation concepts to see daylight and on top of that sometimes the original idea is watered down as it goes through the various departments responsible for delivering on it.

So it takes patience and persistence to see the program come to fruition. Even though executives start with the best intentions, they may not have a good idea about the resources required to make a meaningful and sustainable improvement in the customer experience. Therefore the most common route customer experience leaders and enthusiasts take is to start small, with an early adopter to prove the concept and make the business case.

To make the business case, one obviously needs to measure the right things before and after the change. We had trained an organization on how to do behavioral journey mapping and spoke to them after a while. They said that they did one or two journey mapping projects but then the interest started to fade. When we asked what the results of the project were, we found that they couldn't prove any tangible benefits just because they had not captured the experience and operational metrics before the change.

What defines the success or failure of a CX program is the ability to move the needle on key metrics and prove the benefits to the organization. This takes us to the next critical part: measurement. This is also something that too many organizations don't get right.

Many CX programs are initially positioned as strategic but the energy and enthusiasm fade and with time the program becomes simply about CX metrics tracking. Organizations would say that they measure the customer experience but in most cases, they lack the sophistication necessary to measure it properly and find the key value drivers. All too often the NPS or customer satisfaction is the only CX data available.

As we have explained in this book, our research showed that businesses miss on the biggest driver of value (i.e., emotional attachment). The reason it is not showing on business radars is that most use flawed research methods: looking at what customers say they want and current performance; doing simple correlation or regression and not modeling the whole picture; not including emotions in their research; focusing so much on just one customer experience key performance indicator, that is, NPS®; and mistaking data for insights. We have shown, however, throughout this book that those research methods often produce misleading results.

Forrester's research confirms this. They found that most businesses don't have a clear understanding of the drivers of customer value. Forrester distinguishes between four types of value that customers get from using the products/services of an organization: economic (i.e., think of price, promotions, etc.), functional (i.e., think of ease and speed of accomplishing tasks), experiential (i.e., think about how the customer feels along the journey), and symbolic (i.e., think of the feeling of prestige, pride, socially responsible—the "reflective" (per Dan Norman)—aspect of using the products and services of an organization). Forrester's research shows that the latter two categories are more important but businesses don't know much about them because the data is gathered inconsistently and scattered across different departments, for example, marketing, product, sales, and the CX team. [4]

Fun fact. Just as I'm writing this, I received a message from my mobile service provider asking me to rate how satisfied I'm with their network on a scale of 0 to 10. This is exactly the thing I said is wrong with CX. I really doubt that they have a piece of research with 20, 30, 40, or more aspects of the experience, which include emotional, experiential, and symbolic aspects, and that on top of this list is satisfaction with the network. I think that, because all telecoms measure satisfaction with the network, they have jumped on the bandwagon as well. We've actually done research with telecoms and we know that, if you ask customers what is the most important thing for you, they would say the quality, speed, and reliability of the network (otherwise their phones won't be much useful, would they?). But here's the thing: our research with numerous telecom companies also showed that this is not what drives the most business value, but other things such as feeling respect, feeling valued as a customer, the call center interactions, and the renewal experience. The network? It works just fine 99.99 percent of the time.... Another interesting thing is that when they asked me to rate the network in brackets they put "coverage, quality, and speed of the Internet." So they want me to rate all these three things with just one rating. I wonder what actions this will lead them to!

Speaking of telecoms, a global telecom recently came to us with the same finding. They had hired a contractor to replace someone on maternity leave and the contractor recommended a complete revamp of how they gather customer insights. They found that the survey was asking questions that the company has internal data for and should know the answers to; the survey data was not linked to customer data to allow a more detailed and sophisticated driver analysis and most often the results were considered "out of date" by the time the report was delivered to internal stakeholders. The biggest problem though was that the survey was giving them "tracking data" but really no insights that the product and services teams can use to make changes and improvements that drive growth.

Therefore, it's important to set and track the right metrics (internal operational and external experiential) in order to measure the impact of the customer experience initiatives and also set the program so it facilitates the continuous gathering of actionable customer insights. This should be the foundation of any program. You can't expect to get results if you lack an understanding of the true causes of customer motivation, emotions, and behavior. Nor can you measure your impact and prove the sustainability of the program without the right tracking metrics set in place.

To drive this change, the customer experience function needs a leader. This is another critical part because in our practice we've come across CX directors that were not really leaders. The leader should not only have responsibility but also authority, that is, support from leadership to make things happen and their word should be heard and respected around the organization. In our experience, we have seen people being handed the CX director role who have come from within the organization and have done really well. I recall two instances where people came from a sales background and said that they really liked their new roles and didn't think they could go back to their old jobs. Those were successful in their roles as they knew the organization well and had earned a lot of respect through their careers. Then there is also the option to hire a CX professional.

The leader must be supported by a team because as we've said many times there is a lot of science in customer experience: the science of customer behavior, then there is the science in measurement (i.e., statistics, etc.), then there is the science and art of navigating company politics, leading and managing people through change, and so on. So the leader must be supported by a team, must go through some training and behind-the-scenes tours, and must do quite a lot of reading....

One of the challenges that the CX leader must handle is people saying "why do I need CX, I already know everything I need to know about our clients"; "I know customers, I am a customer myself"; or "it's different for us, customers only buy based on price." The danger here is that people bring their own biases, preferences, and prejudices to the forefront without any credible data that supports them. Therefore it's important to improve their understanding of CX and behavioral science through continuous communication, sharing customer research insights, examples, customer compliments, and, most of all, results. So the team has to take into account that people don't know what they don't know.

I recall a situation where we were at a hospital waiting outside a doctor's office. My partner was at the early stages of her pregnancy. We had just paid for a full package of regular doctor visits and the necessary tests at a private hospital for the duration of her pregnancy. This was her first or second visit. She had made an appointment. She went into her doctor's office but as this happened in the very early days since the hospital opening (it was a brand new branch), there was something about the doctor's ultrasound scanner that was not set so the doctor referred us to another doctor's office down the hall. The problem was that we didn't have an appointment for the doctor's office they referred us to. Not only that but when our doctor told us to go to the other doctor's office, she didn't tell us of any order or put us on a waiting list. So we sat patiently outside the office. We waited about 30 to 40 minutes without anyone giving us any information whatsoever. My partner started to lose patience, so when I saw someone walking out of the office, I asked nicely where on the queue order were we. The doctor answered abruptly, "You are outside the queue order"—meaning we didn't have an appointment. She immediately softened the tone, however, and told us that there are a couple of women ahead of us but expects to see us in 20 to 30 minutes. This answer made my partner stay. I had another appointment and had to leave as this had taken way more than I anticipated. Later in the evening, my partner told me that the doctor was one of the leading professionals in her field and they were using the latest technology. This made me think about the fact that despite all that, earlier that day we were on the brink of leaving the hospital and never coming back. Had we done that, the hospital would have lost not just the money for subsequent visits and tests but also the money related to childbirth. So a significant amount, not to mention all the people we would have told about that bad experience. I notice that one constant question women ask each other when they talk about child-related things is "Where did you give birth?" So word of mouth certainly plays a big role in this sector and they were about to get lots of negative recommendations.

This interaction made me realize again that "people don't know what they don't know." This physician may be a great professional, having spent years of studying and practicing the profession of a gynecologist, but she most probably has not read about the psychology of wait time (i.e., about the fact that unknown wait feels longer than known wait) and I doubt that she reflects too much on the aspects of the patient experience. And I don't think it's her job. It's the job of the chief patient officer and patient experience managers to design an end-to-end experience, act on feedback, and ensure that doctors and staff know not just how to handle health issues but how to handle customer interactions as well. As we gave the example in Chapter 2 with the BATHE method, just a few simple questions can significantly increase patient satisfaction without adding any more time to the interaction. That BAITHE method though is not being taught in medical schools so it takes a dedicated resource to patient experience excellence to turn the doctor's attention to these little things that could make or break an interaction with a patient. This example shows how important the role of the customer experience custodian is in the organization to educate people and push for enhancements to the experience.

This takes me to the thought of Michael Brown, now chief experience officer at Easyenough.com and former chief experience officer at Dick's Sporting Goods. He says that CX should be horizontal, just like the HR function, and not vertical:

> 90–98% of CX initiatives are driven as a vertical. The role of CX is not to drive, not to create new experiences. Just like HR is not about creating new jobs. CX is about facilitating conversations across business units. Customers don't care about org charts, they care about consistent quality experiences

(CQE as he calls them). He says that some executives see CX as a marketing role—to help acquire new customers, some see it as a retention strategy, while others see it as a product and UX. The job of CX executives, he says, is "to break the ego of business unit leaders." "CX executives' role is to bring marketing, product, and service executives together." [5] Although I do believe that customer experience people should be driving the design of experiences, certainly establishing the customer experience function as a horizontal that works with the various departments, brings down silo barriers, and educates and works with the units to achieve the business goals is the right approach.

Another common mistake that we see all too often is that, as is normal for humans to seek simple solutions to our problems, organizations often think that simply buying a new system will improve their experience almost overnight. I remember the time when we were working with a Middle-East telecom. We were meeting various stakeholders and prior to meeting the call center manager, the CX director gave us the heads up that we're likely to hear that the current system they use is mother to all their problems, and a new system will sort things out. Sure enough soon into the conversation, the call center manager started to talk about getting a new system that will improve the experience. I asked him, ok, once you'll get a new system, what are the things that will improve the customer experience and he started to talk about things that had nothing to do with the system, that is, soft skills training and so on. Those were all things that they could be working on even at the moment.

Don't get me wrong: there is nothing wrong with the new systems. And there is nothing wrong with them being pitched as improving the customer experience. The salespeople just respond to the market needs. But there are two things there for me. First, in reality, those systems don't give so much improvement when operated by the same people, recruited and trained in the same way, working in the same noncustomer-centric culture. Second, in a world where there could be technology solutions for pretty much every step of the customer journey, we would advise deploying technology in the area where a technology solution would drive the most value for the customers' experience and the business.

This is exactly the question that a B2B insurance company came to us with. They were about to go through a digital transformation program, completely revamping their digital infrastructure but before they did that they came to us with the basic question "for which experiences do we need to keep the human element, and which should we digitize?" We found that the key value drivers in the experience were the emotional attachment aspects that related to the relationship at a business level and the account management so that was certainly an area where to keep and refocus the human contact. The second biggest value driver area was product-related aspects like the competitiveness of insurance prices, coverage, and flexibility of the policies. Then in third place was something where technology could have made a meaningful difference. Our research found that "responsiveness of claims handling staff" and "being kept informed of the developments of my claim" were also key areas of opportunity. When we journey-mapped the experience we found that this part of the experience can get quite complex with multiple lawyers getting involved for all parties in a potentially long litigation process during which all communication and coordination was largely based on e-mail. This made customers have to follow up and ask for information. It was clear that this is an area where a claims management system, one that would send proactive notifications for status updates and would allow employees, brokers, and clients to log in, read notes, exchange information safely, and communicate, would make a meaningful difference at that stage of the customer journey.

So it's important not to put the cart before the horse. It's important that organizations are clear about the experience they are trying to deliver and source technology that will allow their staff to show that they "know" their customers, to allow them to personalize the experience to customers, to make them feel as valued customers. To achieve this, the organization needs to set a proper CX function, led by a respected professional, and supported by a team that embraces science. They need to implement the right research methods, set the right measurement in place, and educate the board and the organization on what it takes to manage the customer experience. Digital technology can certainly help but if implemented with the right vision about how it would facilitate the desired experience. That new experience should be designed after having found the aspects and moments in the experience that drive the most value to customers and the organization.

A successful customer experience strategy should also be aligned with the brand and marketing. I remember working with a large charge card company, where a manager said: "Marketing has promised customers that we'll take them to the moon and it's my job to tell them there are no tickets to there" (this was back when there were still no commercial flights to Space). In times where spending on digital transformation and marketing technology (martech) is growing at an unprecedented rate, businesses need to ensure that these investments are not turned into missed opportunities. So we'll talk more about these in the next chapters.

As Michael Brown said, the CX function should bring down silos and bring product, marketing, and service people together. Many people see CX as a marketing role, some even say "CX is the new marketing." Our research also showed that Brand & advertising is a key driver of Emotional attachment (see Table 8.1). All too often, however, we see the brand and marketing operating separately from the customer experience and that is another missed opportunity for businesses. In the next chapter, we will discuss how the brand can cultivate an emotional connection with customers.

Practitioner Tips From This Chapter

- Making the business case by (continuously) proving the benefits is key. To do that, one needs to capture and track internal operational metrics, financial metrics, and customer experience metrics at the same frequency so that any changes to these metrics can be attributed to changes in the customer experience and competitive environment.
- Measurement mechanism is one thing, but for continuous improvement, one needs an insights mechanism that feeds them to the product, service, and marketing departments. The organization should put in place a mechanism for the continuous gathering of insights about customer attitudes and behaviors.
- The customer experience should be set as a function, not a short-term budget-led initiative.
- The function needs a leader who doesn't just have responsibilities but the authority to drive changes. The leader should either sit or report to a board member (or the CEO). The leader should be supported by a team.

- A key part of the CX function is to educate the organization and bring down the silos between product, marketing, and service departments.
- The new experience should be designed after having found the aspects and moments in the experience that drive the most value to customers and the organization.

CHAPTER 11

Practice 7

Aim Your Brand at Making an Emotional Connection

People are moving from buying from to buying into

—Mary Portas

As we mentioned in Chapter 8, after we found that Emotional attachment is the biggest driver of value for businesses, I then reanalyzed the data to find which of the traditional touchpoints have the biggest effect on Emotional attachment. First was Customer service with 21 percent, while second came Brand & advertising with 19 percent (see Table 8.1). This shows that through the brand and through advertising, organizations can form an emotional attachment with customers.

Of course, we did not discover America here. In *Psychology Today*, Peter Noel Murray, PhD, highlights four studies of the role of emotion in consumer behavior among which is a functional MRI neuro-imagery research showing that "when evaluating brands, consumers primarily use emotions (personal feelings and experiences) rather than information (brand attributes, features, and facts)." [1]

This is contrary to the predominant advertising theories up until recent years. For most of the 20th century, the belief has been that the role of advertising is to raise brand awareness and persuade the consumer into buying the company's product by conveying the value of the product in the form of information, aiming at the rational thinking activity of the consumer. It has also been assumed that high attention equates to high recall, which equates to high advertising effectiveness.

These two myths are debunked by professor Robert Heath, a senior lecturer at the University of Bath in Great Britain and a long-time innovator in the field of Advertising Theory. Heath and his fellow researchers Drs. Agnes Nairn and David Brandt note in the literature review of their article "Brand Relationships: Strengthened by Emotion, Weakened by Attention," published in the *Journal of Advertising Research* (2006), that the existing theories failed to explain why advertising campaigns that do not convey informational messages have been astonishingly successful. They give the example of a 1992 Renault Clio campaign in the United Kingdom (I've seen that model up close as a family friend of ours had one and was even a passenger once in my youth years). The adverts, some of which you can still find on YouTube, featured affluent French people indulging in that most stereotypical of French activities—flirting and sometimes cheating. The ads show the father ("Papa") giving the keys of the car to his daughter "Nicole," so she could have a ride with or visit her boyfriend, while in some cases the "Papa" is involved with his mistress. The tagline for the ads is "Small car practicality with big car luxury" but it's completely missed as what viewers recall are "Papa" and "Nicole." The ads are being attributed as key to the success of the car. In a market traditionally hostile to French cars, the Clio achieved a 7 percent market share in the small cars segment, surpassing the carmaker's ambitious sales targets by 32 percent. The advertising alone is calculated to have earned Renault some £59 million in additional revenue. [2] What made the advertising successful was the emotional appeal caused by the scenes portrayed, concluded Robert Heath and his team.

A similar case, the authors note, is the story of the Andrex toilet tissue, whose advertising campaigns have featured a small Labrador puppy for several decades. Despite charging higher prices, they have outsold the nearest rival brand by up to 3:1, and this success is attributed to the "emotional appeal of the puppy itself." [3]

Heath and his colleagues find inspiration about deciphering this phenomenon from work in the field of psychotherapy and interpersonal relationships by Paul Watzlawick. Paul Watzlawick was an Austrian-American psychologist, whose career led him to teach psychology at Stanford University in 1967. He is most famous for his work on communication theory (but also credited with introducing the "double bind" theory for schizophrenia). Having also been active in the field of family therapy, Paul and his fellow team of researchers had found that when relationships between couples were on the verge of collapse, the "communication" (i.e., the rational message) was often perfectly reasonable and sensible, but it was the "metacommunication" (i.e., the tone of voice, body language, etc.) that was causing the breakdown. In other words, it was not *what* people were saying (i.e., the rational) that was causing the deterioration of the relationships but *how* they were saying it (i.e., the emotional). Sounds familiar? Robert Heath and his team hence theorize that "in advertising terms, it is not the rational message that builds brand relationships, but the emotional creativity."

To prove this hypothesis they conducted a review of 23 TV advertisements in the United States and 20 in the United Kingdom for a variety of product categories that were run at the time. They administered an online survey among a general population group. To measure the rational argumentation and potency of the ads (i.e., the cognitive power) they asked respondents to evaluate a special set of statements around newsworthiness, differentiation, and factual content. The potency of the emotional content (i.e., the emotive power) in the advertisements was measured using statements based on emotion, mood, and tone. These were then evaluated against the shift in favorability toward the brands (asking customers to rate the brand on a 10-point scale ranging from 1 "extremely favorable" to 10 "extremely unfavorable"). To measure whether or not an ad had produced a shift, a second group of consumers was recruited and asked the favorability question. They were then shown video snippets of the advertisements to establish whether or not they had seen them before and split subsequently into two groups (in roughly the same size). Comparing the brand favorability scores of those who had seen the ads and those who haven't allowed the researchers to establish the "shift in favorability" factor.

The results showed a statistically significant linear relationship with the emotional message and generating a positive brand favorability, while the cognitive message showed no relationship, particularly when controlling for strength of the emotional message. This leads Robert Heath and his team to conclude that those who want their advertising to build strong relationships between the consumer and the brand would be well advised to focus more attention on the emotional metacommunication—the creativity—in their advertisements, than they do on the rational message communication.

But there is a twist and a dilemma to this story.

Do you recall the famous phrase "People will forget what you said, people will forget what you did, but people will never forget how you made them feel." It's credited to the American Poet and civil rights activist Maya Angelou but it may well have its science roots in the work of Paul Watzlawick. One of his most important findings, Robert Heath and his team note, is that "the content of communication (i.e., the message) fades and vanishes over time, whereas the more subtle patterns evoked by the emotional metacommunication endure." The reason for this could be because the "patterns in metacommunication are processed and learned by us automatically, regardless of how much attention we pay." This means that emotional messages will endure, even if processed subconsciously and without active attention. In fact, some researchers,,such as psychologist Robert Bornstein, even suggest that the less aware consumers are of emotional elements in advertising, the better they are likely to work because the viewer has less opportunity to rationally reflect on the message and their future behavior" [4] (i.e., engage in System 2 activity).

So therein lies the dilemma. If advertising has a tactical aim that requires a more rational recall of information, that is, promotion, product performance, website, or phone number recall, it needs consumers to pay more attention. But if it wants to build deeper relationships with consumers and achieve a shift in how they perceive the brand, it needs to incorporate high levels of emotive content, which works best at low attention levels. As you can see, there is as much need for science as for art in advertising.

Still, if you think research based on 43 ads is not representative enough, consider the following findings as well. A Nielson report "Emotions Give a Lift to Advertising" [5] shows the results of a study of 100 ads across 25 brands in the fast-moving consumer goods (FMCG) industry. These ads were grouped into three buckets according to how they scored on a metric based on people's electroencephalogram activity (EEG) while viewing the ad ("Below Average," "Average," and "Above Average"), and using marketing mix modeling, each ad's contribution to sales volume was computed against the average ad for that brand. This test is based on neuroscience and provides the ability to read consumer responses to an ad at both conscious and nonconscious levels. The EEG test detects electrical activity in a person's brain using small, metal discs (electrodes) attached to that person's scalp. Our brain cells communicate via electrical impulses and are active all the time, even when we're asleep. For many researchers, the best way to evaluate emotions is by using techniques that can directly measure neurological and biological reactions, and with the advancement of technology, we can now measure the electrical impulses in specific regions of the brain.

The results showed that ads that generated above-average EEG scores (i.e., with best emotional response) were associated with a 23 percent lift in sales volume over what an average ad would generate (and conversely, below-average ads were associated with a 16 percent decline in sales volume).

There has been an even larger study. Hamish Pringle and Peter Field, authors of *Brand Immortality: How Brands Can Live Long and Prosper* (Kogan Page 2009), dug into the archives of the U.K.-based Institute of Practitioners in Advertising (IPA) dataBANK, which contains 1,400 case studies of successful advertising campaigns. They reported that "campaigns with purely emotional content performed about twice as well (31 percent vs. 16 percent) as those with only rational content" in terms of profitability boost and also did a little better than those that mixed emotional and rational content, that is, 31 percent versus 26 percent. [6]

These studies show that emotion-based advertising content outperforms rational messaging but this doesn't mean that it comes without risks and is a one-size-fits-all type of strategy. As Colin Shaw tends to say, "If it was easy, everyone would be doing it." Pringle and Field point that some brands have damaged themselves when an emotional campaign failed to live with reality and suggest that committing to an emotional branding approach should be "hard-wired into the fabric of the brand," which requires a major commitment as well as a good understanding of consumer motivation. [7] The authors point to Nike's pervasive theme of "success in sport" as an example of a brand that focuses on a key emotional driver and builds advertising, sponsorships, and so on around it.

Emotional creativity, as Robert Heath calls it, may be much more difficult though than just basing a campaign around a "killer fact" (if one is lucky enough to have some). It may also not be such a good fit for brands with low recognition (smaller brands, startups) as it's important not to confuse consumers who don't even associate with the brand and product category. The authors advise small businesses to take the "combined" rational and emotional approach, even if it is slightly less effective, or at least ensure that their emotion-based ads clearly identify the product.

All these studies show that forming an emotional bond with customers by creating more emotive advertising content is the way to go for brand and marketing people and that requires closer cooperation with customer experience people because both teams can benefit from deeper insights into what motivates people to consume the organization's products and services.

Advertising campaigns focusing on emotional content, however, are not the only way brands can build deeper emotional connections with customers and increase sales. Brand messaging around shared values with their customer base is also gaining traction.

I started to think about that when I was sitting at home watching the results of the closely contested 2019 U.S. elections unfold on CNN and kept seeing a Hyundai commercial [8] focused on sustainability. They were not promoting any particular car model, any features, or technology but just spreading the message (in primetime) that they are working toward using sustainable materials. That's a sharp contrast from a car ad that I remember from 2004, which featured a Honda and a Mitsubishi car driving on a bridge and one was able to stop a meter ahead of the other, which was enough not to fall into the collapsed part of the bridge. That was an ad clearly focused on the product aspect of better braking performance (and also probably aiming to tap into the powerful emotion of fear, i.e., fear of getting into a car accident by getting a car with subpar brake performance). Since then, probably knowing about some of the aforementioned research, instead of focusing on product features such as braking or torque, many brands have focused on emotional marketing. BMW's theme was centered around "Joy." Peugeot's (which recently merged with Fiat Chrysler, creating the fourth largest automaker in the world) slogan was "Motion and Emotion," Subaru played with "Confidence in Motion," "Love," "Think, Feel, Drive," and so on. However, Hyundai was onto something else.

Hyundai was trying to capitalize on a trend where more and more consumers want to buy from brands that share the same values as them.

Covid-19 accelerated a shift that has been gradually forming for over 10 years. There has been a global psychological shift in values, beliefs, and needs. Values have evolved, with renewed demands that brands put integrity and purpose before profit. The basis for many customer decisions has shifted. Through Covid-19, the triple bottom line of people, profit, and the planet has become more important than ever.

This trend is evident in data coming out from multiple sources. Accenture Strategy's Global Consumer Pulse Survey 2019 [9] revealed that "65 percent of consumers want businesses to take a stand on issues that are close to their heart." That number rises to 74 percent for 18- to 39-year-olds. And then 43 percent say they would walk away when disappointed by a brand's words or actions on a social issue.

Then, a KPMG Nunwood report [10] from 2020, based on their global Covid-19 tracker, found that 90 percent of customers are willing to pay more for ethical retailers; 56 percent say environmental and social practices of a company have an impact when choosing to buy from them, while 71 percent of customers say if they perceive a brand is putting profit over people they will lose trust in that brand forever.

In other words, consumers say they buy from brands who they share values with.

Research shows Gen Z (born between 1996 and early-mid 2000s) and millennials (Generation Y, born 1981 to 1995) are more inclined to hold brands accountable to their corporate social responsibility goals. You can see that from the Accenture study, and further evidence comes from 5W Public Relations' 2020 Consumer Culture Report. [11] Their research shows that 76 percent of 18- to 34-year-olds like it when CEOs of companies they buy from speak out on issues they care for. This compares to 66 percent of 35- to 54-year-olds and 55 percent of the 55+ age group.

Why is this important? Because Gen Z and millennials now outnumber all other generations globally! This means that this trend has reached a tipping point with a critical mass of people expecting organizations to act with integrity and purpose.

This is all good, but as we have said many times in this book, there is a big difference between what customers say they want and what they do.

In this case though, while some of that may be true to an extent, there is still a critical mass of people that are ready to put their money where their beliefs are. We're seeing a rise in recycling and upcycling and we've got global marches. Another Accenture study [12] found that two-thirds of consumers think their protest actions, including boycotting brands or calling them out on social media, can make a difference in company behavior. Thirty-six percent reported being disappointed by how a company acted, which betrayed their belief in what the company stands for. Nearly half (47 percent) stopped doing business with a company in response to a moment of brand disappointment.

In short, Accenture says "Generations Y (millennials) and Z have ascended to Generation P(urpose)," while KPMG says we've entered into a new age in economy, the "Integrity Economy." However, I like more the definition that Mary Portas gives: "people are moving from buying from to buying into." [13]

What's at stake? According to Accenture, companies will either stand to lose, gain, or retain a piece of the $5 trillion global switching pie. [14]

There are already plenty of examples that this strategy is successful.

Patagonia is one of those. I've started noticing people with their t-shirts even in places where I'd not expect that many people have heard about them. Patagonia says that they are "in business to save our home planet." And they mean it. Their strategy has always been to produce high-quality clothing that doesn't just last one season. They want to reduce textile waste by encouraging customers to either repair their gear or recycle it. [15] Since 1985, Patagonia has pledged 1 percent of sales to the preservation and restoration of the natural environment. They are also an embodiment of what is nowadays called an "activist company." They have fought President Trump on his views on the environment and announced they were giving away the Trump tax cut (estimated at $10M) to environmental causes. They stand against overconsumption and even put an advert for Black Friday with the message "Don't Buy This Jacket." Despite what looks like an antimarketing effort, the company has seen its revenues grow in the face of a challenging environment for traditional retailers. The year the company put out that Black Friday ad (2011), revenue grew by about 30 percent and a further 75 percent between 2013 and 2018. In fact, their revenue grows every time it amplifies its social mission. [16]

Lush is another very good example and a long-time favorite of ours as we've taken customers on our study tours to their shops. Their mission is "to make their products by hand with only vegetarian ingredients and little-to-no preservatives." Why? Because they stand big time against animal testing and cruelty. Lush has been among the top performers in the U.K. Customer Satisfaction Index for many years and has seen tremendous growth globally.

We know what most organizations would say: "it's easy for them because they were founded with these beliefs and purpose in mind." We hear this quite often. However, established organizations like Nike also stand out. When in 2016, quarterback Colin Kaepernick started kneeling during the national anthem before games to protest racial injustice, which effectively ended his NFL career, Nike stood by him. Kaepernick has had a contract with the company since 2011, but it was on the verge of expiration when the company crafted an extension. Then in September 2018, Nike released the advert, titled "Dream Crazy," featuring the former NFL quarterback. The ad read: "Believe in something. Even if it means sacrificing everything. Just do it." A negative reaction was swift and predictable. Videos were uploaded on Twitter of people burning their Nike shoes. Despite the blowback from some Americans, the campaign was deemed a success, and the company's stock rose by 5 percent in the weeks [17] following the advert's release. CBS News even published an article with the headline "Colin Kaepernick Is Nike's $6 billion man," attributing the rise in the stock to Kaepernick's ad, which later went on to win the award for outstanding commercial at the Creative Arts Emmys.

Doing things in a sustainable way doesn't necessarily mean more costs but rather more revenue.

IKEA, for example, set out to be 100 percent powered by renewable energy by 2030, and now generates more renewable energy than it uses.

The retailer has invested in 70,000 solar panels for its stores, selling the extra energy and generating a new revenue stream.

While these may seem like outliers (and perhaps they are to some extent), they fit the broader trend. Kantar Consulting found that brands with a high sense of purpose have experienced a brand valuation increase of 175 percent over the past 12 years compared to the median growth rate of 86 percent. [18]

Let me give one more example, this time from a small business in Eastern Europe. When security forces in Belarus used brutal force and started chasing protesters against President Lukashenko, following an election widely seen as rigged, protesters found shelter in a small cafe. That was until its windows were shattered to pieces by the head of the security forces himself. The next day, Minsk residents helped clean up the glass and have been queuing up outside the O'Petit cafe all day long to show support by buying a cup of coffee. They bought over 300 cups of coffee in the morning alone!

So what does this mean for organizations?

The good news is that now it's actually a good time to showcase your values, purpose, and integrity. According to Google research, 84 percent of U.S. consumers say that how companies or brands act during the Covid-19 market is important to their loyalty moving forward. [19]

Leading organizations know this and have moved to action. Uber, which has been working very hard to build customer trust in recent years, has committed to providing 10 million rides and food deliveries to health care workers and people in need, free of charge. Dyson in the United Kingdom turned from manufacturing vacuum cleaners and hand driers to making ventilators at scale. LVMH, the owner of Louis Vuitton, Moët Hennessy, Givenchy, Christian Dior, and many more brands, was manufacturing hand sanitizer rather than perfume.

Marriott is another good example. I got an e-mail with the subject line "A message from our CEO" in mid-March 2019 that basically communicated all the steps they are taking to ensure health and safety, extending the time to redeem points, changes to the cancellation policy, and so on. Communication in those times was important. But what was more impressive was the follow-up e-mail about three weeks later titled "An update from our CEO." Right at the top was a section "In the Community." Here are some of the things in there:

> Around the world, our hotels located in close proximity to hospitals are in a unique position to help. Many of these properties are providing respite to weary hospital workers, military personnel and supermarket employees who need to stay close to work or are concerned about going home to their loved ones. In Suzhou, China, associates at five Marriott brand hotels found another way to help first responders. When a local surgical mask factory announced that it needed workers, about 30 of our associates volunteered to help manufacture and package the masks. ... It's that kind of spirit that will sustain us through this crisis.

Of course, there are hundreds of similar stories from the pandemic and post that. Airbnb has said it will temporarily house 20,000 Afghan refugees, fleeing the Taliban regime, at no charge to help them resettle across the world. I also like a story from before Covid-19. Dawn dish soap was hailed as a wildlife rescue hero for cleaning hundreds of birds after the Gulf Coast oil spill in 2010. Consumers viewed the brand with pride for being part of the overall humanitarian response to this ecological disaster. And since then, the brand has featured a fluffy baby-bird (looks like a baby-duck to me) on its products.

In case this reminds you of the Andrex toilet paper, we need to answer why people like pictures of puppies, fluffy little bears (that have little to do with actual bears), and fluffy baby ducks. Paul J. Zak, the professor of economic sciences, psychology, and management in Claremont Graduate University's Division of Politics & Economics, whom we mentioned in Chapter 8, comes with the answer.

Professor Zak and his team played a story to study participants about a boy with cancer and his father going through emotional ups and downs about trying to join his son in his joyfulness while knowing that he is dying. As participants experienced the story, their brains produced cortisol, a hormone associated with distress but also making you pay more attention, and oxytocin, a hormone that promotes social connection, care, and empathy. Participants were then given the option to share money with a stranger and those who produced the most oxytocin were the most likely to give money to others they couldn't see. [20] In a different study, participants were infused (intranasally) with a dose of oxytocin and that proved to increase their generosity by 80 percent. [21] Because oxytocin receptors in the human brain are "preferentially located in areas associated with emotions and social behaviors (especially the amygdala, hypothalamus, and anterior cingulate), this suggests a role for emotions in supporting generosity," the researchers say. Then, in yet another but similar experiment, participants, after sniffing oxytocin or the placebo, were made to watch short public service announcements that had aired on television in the United States and the United Kingdom. The results were similar: study participants who received oxytocin donated 56 percent more and also reported that the advertisements made them feel more empathetic. "Our results show why puppies and babies are in toilet paper commercials. This research suggests that advertisers use images that cause our brains to release oxytocin to build trust in a product or brand, and hence increase sales," Zak says. [22] So there you have it. The images we see affect the chemicals in our brain, and images of puppies and fluffy baby animals release oxytocin (the social connection and empathy hormone), which unconsciously makes us connect with the brand. But as Robert Heath's research suggested, this all depends on the level of (conscious) attention we pay to these subliminal messages. The more attention we pay the less effective they are. The reason for that is the more attention we pay, the more we engage our Rational System and the more we reason, the more we think about whether something is worth the price or not, whether we need it, we compare different products, and so on.

What do organizations need to do?

Aim for an emotional connection. The businesses that can connect with people as people, not merely consumers, will start generating a whole new way of shopping. This can be done through the design of the customer journey and also through the brand and marketing. Since we talked mostly about the latter in this chapter, we'll focus more on that aspect.

Define what social and environmental issues you as a company care about. Think of a multiyear plan about how to make change happen. Some go even as far as to think in terms of a 30-year framework. Such is Lorna

Davis, former CEO of the multibillion-dollar organic consumer packaged goods (CPG) conglomerate DanoneWave, who counts Patagonia's CEO Rose Marcario as a close adviser. She pushes those around her to work on a "30-year framework," to understand the long-range consequences of business decisions, rather than merely what will move the needle next month or next year.

Think of the entire ecosystem. Think about the well-being and engagement of your employees. As we've said in Chapter 9, when we at Beyond Philosophy have been advising clients on the emotions they want to target in their customers, we've been also saying to them that they need to target the same emotions with employees: (a) so employees don't see the organization as cynical but also (b) so they can see what it means to evoke and feel these emotions.

The same goes for customers. Organizations need to plan for an emotional connection with customers. Especially now, as more and more journeys are now digital, organizations should not just think in terms of process steps (i.e., click here first, enter this info, then click here). They should also plan on designing an emotionally engaging experience along the customer life cycle journey.

An important consideration in this new "integrity economy" should also be given to the suppliers. We've seen the backlash when it turns out that a supplier has used child labor in the production of the products or makes employees work in inhumane labor conditions.

This works both ways. Everyone's brand is being redefined right now based on their actions, the actions of leadership, the actions of employees, the actions of suppliers.

In summary, organizations need to find ways to connect with their customer base on issues they care for, show them through communications that these are front and center of what they do as a company, and above all make them real through the experience they deliver.

This just shows how interconnected the brand and the customer experience are. Through brand communications, social media interactions, sponsorships (think of Red Bull), and advertising, the brand can influence customer perceptions and, vice versa, when customers actually have experiences interacting with the organizations, they can change those perceptions (for good or bad) and influence the perceptions of others.

As a matter of fact, a Chief Marketing Officer (CMO) Council survey asked the C-suite to answer the question, "What do you consider to be the essential role of a CMO in your executive team?" [23] At the top of the list, with 62 percent was the expectation of the CMO to be "customer experience advocate and champion," followed by "digital transformation/ marketing automation leader" (we'll talk about that in the next chapter), "brand reputation custodian and value creator," "maestro of communication and demand generation," and fifth, with 40 percent, was "customer insights authority (360-degree view)."

I also believe in those #1 (customer experience champion) and #5 "customer insights authority" roles. The two are of course interconnected too. As we have said and showcased many times in this book, organizations need to get to a deeper level of insights that are not based just on rational answers (i.e., what customers say they want) but go into a deeper level, into the emotional and subconscious drivers. Those could be found, depending on the objective and setting, using advanced predictive analytics, using machine learning (ML) and AI technologies, through Implicit Association Tests (that measure the speed of reaction/association), behavioral conjoint analysis, in-depth customer interviews, and so on. These research methods can be useful to both the brand, to understand how people perceive the brand, and the products—what are their motivators for using their products and services and what are the perceived barriers to using them. Those advanced research methods can be also used by customer experience practitioners, who are trying to improve the experience, build a stronger connection with customers, and drive growth just like the brand people want to do.

In many instances, the executive sponsor for our projects working with big companies had been the CMO or equivalent. However, there had also been instances where the brand people are coming to meetings just as observers, to make sure we don't step on their turf or, in some instances, they had been working with their own advisor, developing brand personalities and content that is not based on the same in-depth research as we did working on the customer experience project.

Therefore, there is a need for more alignment and a data-driven approach—an approach that makes a fusion between technology, data, and customer knowledge (behavioral science). We believe that this will be the key to competitive advantage in the future. That future is now as there are already pioneer companies who have created this kind of fusion. We'll discuss this, the digital transformation, the use of AI and data, in the final three chapters of this book (Part III: The Tomorrow of CX Management and How to Get There).

Practitioner Tips From This Chapter

- The brand could be a powerful driver of emotional bonding with customers.
- Share insights about customers in the different stages of the sales funnel and customer life cycle between departments (i.e., brand & marketing, product, customer experience, customer service, etc.).
- Strive for emotive content in advertising and publications (this may vary or be mixed with rational content depending on the type of business, the situation, and objectives).
- Have a higher purpose as an organization, share, live, and communicate your values to connect with the new generation of customers.

PART III

The Tomorrow of CX Management and How to Get There

In Part I of this book we shared research about the important role emotions play when it comes to driving business value and how this is largely an untapped opportunity as most organizations don't have a coherent and science-based strategy on how to create an emotional attachment with customers. In Part II of the book, we discussed some of the components of such a strategy. So far, however, the studies, examples, and advice we have given were based on past data and experiences. The world, however, does not stay static and keeps changing and evolving. So we need to look at what will be key for customer experience management and customer-driven growth in the future.

Today more and more experiences are turning digital; more and more investment is poured into digital transformation initiatives, martech, and AI solutions. This trend had started years ago and was even more accelerated by the pandemic. It is clear that these are not just temporary phenomena but will shape the future of customer experience. More digital experiences mean a lot more data about customers and their behavior online. That can be analyzed using AI and then used by marketing and brand people to drive conversion and emotional attachment with the brand or by customer experience people to drive higher retention and product usage, implementing various behavioral science nudges along the way. Organizations that create this fusion between technology, data, and customer science will have a competitive advantage.

There is one "however," though. AI is only as good as the data it uses to learn and the purpose it's been given. Technology and processes will be as good as the design intent that made them see daylight. If executives and organizations as a whole do not have a very good understanding of the drivers of customer behavior, could they solve their business problems with digital transformation and AI? We already provided evidence from our research and from that of others that emotional attachment is the key driver of business value. We explained some of the psychology behind this phenomenon. Yet, we know that most organizations don't have a strategy that addresses customer emotions. Therefore, if organizations lack an understanding of what really drives customer attitudes and behavior there is a real danger that they will miss a big opportunity to turn their investments in digital transformation into a driving force of customer engagement and competitive advantage.

In Part III of this book—"The Tomorrow of CX Management and How to Get There"—we will discuss how to make the best use of digital technology and what are the pitfalls to avoid.

In Chapter 12, "The Problem With Digital Transformation Today," we will look at why many digital organizations fail to deliver results and what are the critical questions to answer when setting the strategy for their digital transformation program. Next, in Chapter 13, "AI and the Future of Customer Experience," we will discuss how organizations can use AI not just to automate interactions but to drive deeper customer insights and improve customer experience. Finally, in Chapter 14, "The Rise of Customer Science Teams," we will paint a picture of what the future of customer experience management holds for us and how some organizations are using the power of technology, AI, data science, and behavioral science in the design of the experience.

CHAPTER 12

The Problem With Digital Transformation Today

Companies have the desire for revolution, but the stomach for evolution.

—Michael Brown

One of our clients, a water company in the United Kingdom, told us in the mid-2010s that they were looking to go through a digital transformation and they were particularly looking to expand the Facebook and Twitter channels as a way for customers to contact them. So when we were doing research they were very keen on specifically asking questions about the different contact channels: phone, webchat, and social media. The research found that contacting the company by web and social media doesn't drive value and in the discussions, we found that 94 percent of contacts come on the phone. When we looked at why that is the case, we found that many of the contacts are for things like a blocked sewer. Now, if your toilet is blocked, would you brag about it on social media or would you pick up the phone and try to get it sorted ASAP? We found that there were other ways where technology could improve the customer experience, but inviting customers to report issues through social media was not going to give them the uplift they expected.

I think that this story is symptomatic of how people approach digital transformation. In many instances, they approach it with some preconceived ideas without the necessary data and insights to derive business value from the investment.

Digital transformation is what has been keeping executives up at night for the last few years and when Covid-19 hit, it became the #1 business objective for most organizations.

The search on the term "digital transformation" has grown at least 400 percent in the last five years, while spending on digital transformation projects has grown by 54 percent ($700 billion) between 2018 and 2019 alone.

McKinsey says, the potential uplift from doing digital transformation in a way that improves customer experience is 20 to 30 percent improvement in customer satisfaction, which in turn could lead to 20 to 50 percent more economic gains. [1] Yet, McKinsey also reports that 70 percent of digital transformation projects do not reach their stated objectives. [2] Based on the $1.3 trillion estimated spend on digital transformation in 2018, it equates to over $900 billion worth of spend that will miss the mark. [3] For 2019, it was estimated that 40 percent of all dedicated technology spending was for digital transformation, which means companies have spent more than $2 trillion on it, putting up to $1.4 billion investment in jeopardy.

The problem is not that organizations shouldn't invest in technology. Most organizations are wary about the future challenges associated with competing with companies that are "born digital" and the risks to their operating and business models as more and more customer experiences and interactions are now digital.

However, businesses should realize that customers don't opt for one company's products and services over another because one is new and digital, but because of the value they get or don't get. As we've said in previous chapters, in broader terms, customers get value in four ways: economic (more narrowly this is about the cost of products and services but it could be broader than that as well, i.e., competitive transit times if we take the logistics industry as an example), functional (i.e., the ease and convenience of completing tasks/jobs, the speed at doing so, etc.), experiential (this is about the experience the organization provides and how it makes customers feel), and symbolic (this is about the status feeling customers get when using the products and services of an organization). Interestingly, Forrester says that the latter two categories are more important value drivers/dimensions. [4]

In other words, customers will leave you because of the experience you provide to them and the ability to achieve their goals and objectives (both functional and emotional, personal, and business related) using your products and services. So it is most important to understand the value drivers in the experience and understand how technology can help you to deliver more value to customers and streamline your operations. Finding the value drivers would also mean that you "do not throw the baby out with the bathwater," as Colin Shaw, the CEO of Beyond Philosophy, would often say, by automating the wrong thing or removing the human element from a place where it was adding value.

Here is an example of what I mean. This was one of the findings from a recent project with an energy supplier that I mentioned earlier in the book. They had acquired different brands and for various reasons (probably to do with cost savings) they had decided to change the way they would take orders from their commercial customers. Instead of ordering from the local branch by phoning their contact or dropping by the local office, the company decided to direct business customers to a 1-800 central number. With this, however, they took away the feeling of a relationship with the organization that customers had, the recognition of being long-term customers (symbolic value), and the joyful experience of talking to a local contact whom they've known for many years (experiential value). This led to many customers voicing their frustration, some by simply walking out and choosing another supplier. When making the change, at least they had to consider how to preserve that feeling of a relationship and recognition using technology. They could have ensured that through technology that allows them to recognize who the business contact is, how long they have been a customer and, on a more practical level, what instructions they need to pass to the drivers in order to make a delivery to a remote place in Canada. But, as we have said, most businesses do not focus on and think in terms of customer emotions, and therein lies the *big miss*.

If the objective of deploying technology is just to save costs by automation, it is fine. It will ensure that your cost base stays competitive and you can offer economic value. In this case, organizations should be just wary of not automating and removing the human element from an interaction, where it was driving value to customers and consequently to the organization. Customers leaving or calling the contact center en masse to solve issues may significantly skew the technology ROI calculations. Forrester's research, however, as we said earlier, shows that it's the experiential and symbolic value dimensions that are more important.

Therefore it is no surprise that one of the commonly stated objectives of the application of digital technology is precisely to improve the customer experience. However, the results show that more often than not, that doesn't happen. So why is that the case?

Do executives just pay lip service to customer experience or do they fall into the trap of the "shiny new object"? Is it in the implementation when things go wrong or it's just the fact that people don't know what they don't know (i.e., all the science and psychology related to customer experience and customer research)?

Evidence that the customer experience is not front and center of digital transformation efforts comes from a global survey of 800 chief information officers (CIOs) by Dynatrace where 73 percent of respondents said the need for speed in digital innovation is putting customer experience at risk. And nearly two-thirds (64 percent) of CIOs admitted they are forced to compromise between faster innovation and the need to ensure customers have a great experience. [5]

Then, as we discussed in Chapter 10 about why some customer experience programs fail, people (that means executives too) have the tendency to seek simple solutions to complex problems and tend to fall for the "shiny new object" syndrome, that is, fall in love with the technology that is being sold to them. This is putting the cart before the horse.

What do organizations that achieve their digital transformation goals do differently than organizations that achieve average results?

The recently published report "The 2021 State of Digital Transformation" by Altimeter, a research and consulting firm owned by Prophet, sheds some light. They surveyed 587 executives from the United States, Europe, and China across a range of industries about their digital capabilities, the key investments, and the choices they made that got them to where they are. By separating the responses of high performers and average performers, they were able to draw some insights as to what factors lead to the success of digital transformation initiatives. The definition for a high performer in their research was whether or not the respondent rated the success of their digital transformation program as excellent, where excellent meant that they have met or exceeded all of their digital transformation goals within the timeframe they expected.

Aim for Growth and Innovation

A cornerstone finding in the Altimeter report is that high-performing companies' goal for their digital transformation program is growth and innovation and they measure success with business performance metrics (revenue, profit, etc.), while average performing companies are far more focused on reducing operating costs and measure success with operational efficiencies. [6] Organic growth can be improved by (1) improving customer acquisition through better use of data and artificial intelligence (AI) to optimize and personalize the marketing of the company's products and services. We'll touch on this later in this chapter and in the next chapter where we'll talk about how marketing technology and AI are revolutionizing this field. Then organic growth can also be achieved by (2) innovations in improving the customer experience, thus increasing retention and spend and generating customer referrals and innovations in products and services. The starting point for these growth strategies should be data: data about the intrinsic motivators (conscious and unconscious) for customers to pay for the organization's products and services, the perceived barriers to using them, and the customers' unmet needs. All of this data should be segmented by types of customers in order to find the niches where innovations can drive financial returns.

The first critical question the organization should aim to answer right at the start of its digital transformation program is:

1. *What drives value for customers and the organization?*
   Organizations need to find the key drivers of customer behavior, the customers' unmet needs by the organization and in the marketplace as a whole, the interactions that create value, that create dissatisfaction, and the underlying causes for these interactions. Finding unmet customer needs in the organization's experience and proving that would drive value for the organization would be an area for innovation and improvement in the experience. However, finding an unmet customer need in the marketplace would be an area for competitive differentiation and would bring the advantage of a first mover in the space. Organizations can use a variety of methods for finding the key value drivers depending on the settings, customer

journey, and so on. They can use predictive driver analytics and ML algorithms for large data sets, in-depth customer interviews, and so on.

Then, the next critical question is:

2. *What experiences should be digital, where could technology improve the experience and drive savings, and where should the human element be redeployed?*

Answering the first question will highlight the areas where technology can drive the most improvement to the customer experience and ROI. In some instances, these could be small-scale changes at different points in the customer journey while in others it may be one big technology-enabled change at a key moment in the customer journey. Earlier in the book, we gave an example about an insurance company that came to us with the question, "Where should we automate things and where should we retain or redeploy the human element?" We found the areas where it was the human element that was driving the most value for the organization and an area where a technology solution will bring value and improve the efficiency of the process and the customer experience.

Another more radical change example is the Amazon Go store. They have completely redesigned the convenience store concept and to an extent the business model. We visited their first Amazon Go store in Seattle within days of opening doors. When we went, there were even tourists (mostly Asian) taking photos outside and we too didn't miss the chance. For those, not having been to one, the process is as follows. Upon arrival there, you can download and register on the Amazon Go app using the store's free wifi (unless you've done this ahead of time of course). Then you scan the app as you go in, grab what you want, put it in the bag, and scan the app as you go out. There are no cashiers. They even tell you "Seriously, you can go out" (that is the last screen on the "how it works" app instructions) because they had found that when simply leaving shoppers were feeling like shoplifters. Using a number of sensors, once you take an item and put it in your bag, it automatically gets checked in your digital shopping bag as well. Shortly after you leave the store you get your receipt, containing the items in your bag with pictures and the prices. Of course, this is already paid with the credit card you associated with the app. However, having no cashiers doesn't mean having no employees. They had just moved employees from less value-adding activities (to the customer and the business) to more value-adding activities. Instead of sitting on a chair or behind the counter most of the time, scanning barcodes, employees are moved to the shop floor where they help customers find the products they are looking for and provide advice when needed. The other job function they perform is stocking the shelves. I noticed that the shelves appeared smaller, there were quite a few empty stock rows (which I attribute to the overwhelming interest, being new in this business and getting to know the amount of demand for various items), but of course, Amazon being Amazon, instead of apologizing, they put their smiley logo arrow with the sign "so good it's gone." The store's square footage also appeared smaller than a typical convenience shop. This made me think that by diverting the human labor to more stocking activities, they can also use less square footage and generate more sales per square foot, saving costs on rent.

Here is the most interesting part though. I noticed that on top of the receipt they had put the amount of time I had spent in the store. I think that by doing that they want to show customers the functional value they get, that is, really quick shopping, in and out of the store in no time. After all, that's what convenience is, isn't it!

So, businesses could rethink their business models, now that technology allows them to do things that appeared unthinkable before. They need to understand what customers' unmet needs are, what is driving their behavior and emotional attachment, and decide how they will provide value for customers and the organization in the future. Then, they can source the technology that will allow them to implement their vision for the experience.

Once the organization has decided how to use technology and which experiences to be digital, the next critical question is as follows:

3. *How do we make digital experiences emotion-aware?*

What organizations should be well aware of is that technology per se is highly unlikely to evoke the desired emotions in customers. The experience needs to be thought through, the technology to be adapted and it'll be the little things that create those emotions. How do you know if your new experience creates the desired emotions? By testing it! We spoke about Stanford d.School's approach to design when we shared Doug Dietz's story about the little girl and the MRI scan. What we said back then was that one of the things we liked most about that methodology was the fact that it ends with "Test." How do you test the new design? The good news is that for assessing a digital experience, there are some pretty handy and robust methods. For once, people can just record a video of themselves and their screen (they can do that on their mobile, tablet, or desktop computer) while going through your digital experience (conducting a task that you had given them, e.g., file a claim, book a stay). Analyzing that video with facial emotion recognition cloud-based AI analytics will show you what emotions customers feel at each millisecond of their experience. If they do that using technology that captures where their eyes are glazing, then bingo. You would know where do your website visitors look first; second, how long their eyes gaze on an item, which kind of visual information do they ignore (but are supposed to respond to); does an individual's gaze return to a visual element that was looked at before, and so on. And if you combine this with a watch-looking wrist device that measures the GSR, you'd be able to measure the intensity of the emotional arousal.

This way an organization can test its new digital experience design and find where to make tweaks to improve the design and elicit the desired value-driving customer emotions. They can also test various behavioral science nudges to see which ones increase conversion, engagement, and provide value to customers.

The Altimeter report, we mentioned earlier, found that high-performing organizations were more likely to focus on customer experiences than other companies and thus a "customer-focused transformation, rather than tech- or process-focused transformation was more likely to drive success." The three critical questions that we discussed previously will ensure that your digital transformation program remains customer-focused and would drive value for customers and the organization.

Those are not the only success factors though....

Aim for a Coordinated Effort

One thing is to talk about a real digital transformation and another is to implement piecemeal changes and process automation here and there and give it a fancy label. Real digital transformation often means changes to the business model and sacrificing some "sacred cows" (i.e., product/service offerings; what and how much the company charges for) to future-proof revenue streams and this requires a coordinated effort. The other thing that often happens is that some programs simply are not going far enough to improve the customer experience. Michael Brown, the former customer experience director of Dick's Sporting Goods, whom we've mentioned earlier in the book and who has also worked on digital transformation at SAP, says: "Companies have the desire for *revolution*, but the stomach for *evolution.*" He says that a company he worked with had attempted to change their system 14 times, but it never happened. "It was always an evolution, not a revolution," he says, until one day they completely changed their approach to transformation. Often, the reason for that, he says, is "because of social pressures" (i.e., if you do this you would disrupt how X department is doing their work and someone might be out of a job, etc.). [7]

In the past, businesses used to take a "toe in the water" approach to digital transformation where the efforts were focused on one department first before being sequentially scaled to others but now organizations can't afford any delays. There needs to be a holistic and coordinated approach that spans across departments such as marketing, sales, and service. Those should be supported by a common digital infrastructure that facilitates the gathering of data, leveraging it to gain insights and sharing it across different functions within the organization.

This can only happen if senior leadership embraces the idea of a holistic change to how the organization operates. It needs to start with the business strategy first and be led by the executive team. Some would argue that, in order to oversee the different workstreams, it needs its own chief executive (i.e., transformation officer), as the CEO's job is to lead the organization, but Altimeter's survey data suggests that most successful digital transformations are led by the CEO. The CEO has the clout and credibility to lead the transformation efforts as he/she is the custodian of the company's vision and higher purpose. Furthermore, no other executive has access to more resources or the ability to galvanize all departments to work toward a shared vision of the future than the CEO. Regardless of whether it's the CEO or a chief digital officer that leads, all board members must be involved. Michael Brown also says that it needs to be driven as a horizontal and not a vertical initiative.

Aim for Employee Engagement

The other must-do for a digital transformation, that most people agree on, is recognizing employees' resistance to change and fears that their jobs may be put on the line. Learning to use collaboration tools, technology upgrades requiring employees to improve their digital skills, hierarchy reorganizations—all these things cause anxiety in employees. It is therefore important to engage them early on in the process and leverage their knowledge of internal system deficiencies and what causes dissatisfaction in customers. Then you can engage them in the redesign of the experience.

The next crucial phase is implementation and that should go with a thought-through change management program, which addresses employees' fears associated with the change and potentially the reskilling required. To go through this, employees need to know that transformation is not just done for the sake of transformation and cutting costs. Organizational leaders must clearly convey the vision and purpose of the transformation and the expected benefits. Focusing on those key for the employee experience emotions that we discussed in Chapter 8 will ensure employees remain engaged and committed throughout the change process.

Aim for the Right Martech

Marketing is also an area that is going through a transformation and heavily investing in technology (nicknamed "martech"). The CMO Council reports that nearly 70 percent of its members are increasing their investments in marketing technology and martech is a $122 billion industry that's growing by 22 percent year over year. [8] And they too are struggling to make those investments pay off.

Carl F. Mela, professor of marketing at Duke University, and Brian Cooper, senior director of demand, analytics, and information at Juniper Networks, write in their HBR article "Don't Buy the Wrong Marketing Tech" that organizations often fail to consider what data would really help their marketing efforts and don't consider how the technology they are buying would work with other technologies in the organization. The two main culprits they name for failing to make those martech investments work are "data hoarding" and the "shiny new object" syndrome. It's a quite good article and I'd encourage you to read it. We already spoke about the "shiny new object syndrome" and the fact that often people put the cart before the horse when we discussed customer experience programs failures, so let me address the "data hoarding" aspect because that will lead us into the final two chapters of this book.

A few years ago, I was working with a bank and did a journey mapping project on their mortgage experience. One of the things I showed them was how complex and how much information they ask on their initial paper application. For example, one of the fields you had to complete was about the kind of car you had. I know what you might be thinking, that it could be used as something that could be mortgaged too in case of a need. But I've never even heard of such a case from anyone and certainly wasn't going to apply to my case. When speaking with mortgage consultants you learn that there are two basic things that they need to establish, that is, how much you earn (there are two questions related to this: How much is the salary on which you pay national insurance? How much you actually earn—through dividends, rent, profit if you have your own company, etc.?) and how much you spend on other loans, rent, and so on. These two will give them your disposable income figure. Of course, having savings, credit cards, and so on are also factors. Then they ask you how much is the property you want to buy and how much you want to borrow (i.e., how much will be your own contribution to the purchase). These are also pretty much all the fields you need to complete in the digital form. As you can see, nowhere in this is a car model being mentioned. The executives were all blown away by how many irrelevant aspects and friction points there were in the experience and all agreed this form was one of those, as they knew very well that they didn't do anything with that data. As we've said before in this book, there is nothing like going and seeing the real experience firsthand!

Later, when I was training a group of their mid-level managers on key aspects of customer experience and how to use journey mapping to map and redesign an experience, at some point, I gave them the aforementioned form as an example of not really seeing things from the customers' perspective. I remember how one of their employees challenged me on that car question in their form with the words "data is gold." And who could blame him? Just the other day, my eyes gazed at an HBR article with the heading "Data is fuel of the new economy." Yes, data is gold and fuel to the new economy but only if you do something with it and capitalize on it.

Asking customers to give you data just for the sake of hoarding it and not doing anything with it, let alone providing value back to customers, is just a pure punishment for customers. Carl F. Mela and Brian Cooper make the analogy that it's like "collecting hay to find needles" and that's not very efficient. The companies are sitting on tons of data on website traffic, browsers, devices used to access their servers, call center interactions, lots of voice recordings of calls for quality control purposes; they also have the capability to purchase more data from external providers like Experian. So hoarding just for the sake of it would mean that much of this data may be irrelevant and distracting. When data hoarding is not goal directed, the authors argue, "that's a problem that even predictive artificial intelligence can't solve." Instead, what businesses need to do is to start with a business objective in mind and work out what data they would need to solve it, how and where they can gather that data, and how to use AI as one of the tools in their arsenal to help them achieve their objective.

This takes us to the next critical capability for the sustainability of the customer experience and digital transformation programs and future competitiveness of organizations.

Aim to Develop Data as a Strategic Asset

The biggest capability gap between top performers in digital transformation and average performers, that the Altimeter survey found, was in their use of data. Top performing organizations were far more likely to say that they are deriving continuous and compounding value from data

(39 percent) compared to average performers (10 percent). They were also more likely to use AI to generate predictive analytics that can be used to design real-time customer experiences (35 percent) than average performers (12 percent). This highlights that effective use of data is key and tapping into the opportunities that AI provides will be vital for the next phase of digital transformation and the competitiveness of the organization in the future. We will look into this in depth in the next two chapters.

In summary, organizations need to start their digital transformation initiatives by finding the key value drivers in the experience, mapping and reimagining it for the future, and then see how technology can help and turn their vision of what the experience should look like into a reality. Then test the new design.

Of course, for something as complex as digital transformation, you need more than this to make it a success and achieve the business objectives. If an IT specialist was writing this book, he/she would be talking about IT architecture, data warehouses, and so on. If a change management specialist was writing this book he/she would write about—you guessed it—change management, the need for tracking and reporting tools, and so on. If an HR person was writing it, he/she would talk about the importance of engaging employees, the skills needed, and so on. And they would all be right.

When there is no silver bullet, it takes a plethora of factors for a successful digital transformation. Different people will create different listings with the must-dos for a successful digital transformation, but for one thing, they all agree. If the goal of the transformation is to improve the customer experience and align the digital initiatives to customer experience strategy, then it needs to be preceded by a diagnostic phase where customer insights are gathered.

There are many elements to a successful digital transformation program, but starting with the customer insights as to what would provide value for customers in a future experience, setting the right structure and executive support, and managing the people side of things are three essential elements for achieving the business goals.

How organizations develop data as an asset and leverage AI to drive growth and improve the customer experience in the digital age will be discussed in the next chapter.

Practitioner Tips From This Chapter

When going about digital transformation:

- Find the key value drivers (rational, emotional, subconscious) and unmet needs in the experience.
- Decide which interactions to automate, where to deploy technology, and where to keep or redeploy the human element.
- In the design of the experience, think of how to design it so it still elicits the key value-driving emotions, even if it's automated.
- Test the new design with behavioral simulations or using techniques that can directly measure neurological and biological reactions (heart rate, sweat, posture, facial reactions, etc.).
- If it is a big organizational change it needs the right structure and executive support. It needs to address not just the technology but the people side of change too.
- Aim for a coordinated effort, one that spans across departments but is led by the top. Aim to develop data as a strategic asset and leverage the power of AI predictive analytics (for that we'll talk more in the next chapter).

CHAPTER 13

AI and the Future of Customer Experience

Integrate data science with behavioral science and ask the right questions from the beginning in order to get the most out of the data. Embrace AI to mine the data and engage Behavioral Science to interpret the data.

—Cerita Bethea

Nowadays it's not uncommon for companies to be sitting on large masses of customer data from customer interactions (digital and in-store) or in the form of customer profiles. That also includes the millions of recorded phone calls for the occasional "training and development purposes." In addition, there are now widely available third-party data sets with customer profile descriptors including attitudes, digital and social media behaviors, as well as biometric data from wearable devices that includes health data, location data, and so on. While big data was the buzzword a whole decade ago it is only in the last few years that advancements of ML algorithms and cloud-based solutions gave rise to a plethora of artificial intelligence (AI) solutions that help organizations analyze those enormous data sets, find nonobvious insights, and uncover competitive advantages.

Organizations are asking themselves, "Why use a survey to ask customers about their experiences and preferences when data about customer interactions can be used to predict both satisfaction and the likelihood that a customer will purchase again?"

Given what we've discussed in length in this book about customers giving you potentially deceiving answers and not really being aware of what drives their behavior, you might be thinking that AI is the answer to all your questions that keep you awake at night. Not so fast though. In some cases, it may indeed do wonders for your organizational growth so in this chapter we'll review some instances of successful AI applications but by now, given what we discussed in the previous chapter, you should be aware that the shiny new object is not always the silver bullet people are hoping for. So we'll talk about how AI can be used and how to supplement it with other methods to get actionable insights.

Organizations' path to organic growth goes through increasing the value of their customer base either through augmenting it (i.e., customer acquisition), through deepening customer relationships, and increasing the average revenue per customer (think of cross-selling, purchasing premium packages, increasing usage, etc.), or through increasing customer retention (with evidence suggesting that the latter costs a lot less and provides exponential benefits to the bottom results).

We will look at how AI can be used to help customer acquisition, deepen customer relationships, and increase retention.

AI Use in Customer Acquisition

The CMO Survey (2020) reports a "low level of contribution of marketing analytics to firm performance and no improvement in that contribution over the last eight years." [1] We already provided evidence about firms falling in love with the wrong martech and this is yet even more evidence about the disconnect between marketing data growth and firm growth. But there are some success stories too. One of those is from a company called Quantcast, which helps organizations to profile their customer base and find the behavioral patterns that lead to conversions. Quantcast builds a custom model using millions of data points available about the customers (e.g., demographics, presearch behaviors, past purchases) and finds the drivers of conversion. Then, they find audiences that fit this profile and deliver the organization's message to them at the "perfect time." With their targeted audience selection, Quantcast was able to bring prospects to IKEA's website that were 16 times more likely to buy something than average IKEA site visitors. [2] This is just one of many examples of firms employing AI-powered analytics to fine-tune their targeting and lower the cost per acquisition. One note of caution here is that brands should be wary of focusing too much on lower-funnel actions (i.e., price promotions and personalized deals in real time) at the expense of upper-funnel actions (e.g., brand building). While the former may be easier to measure and bring immediate results, throughout this book we have provided abundant evidence of the benefits of creating an emotional attachment with the brand and the financial effects over the long term.

Another useful application of AI technology is facial emotion recognition. As we have shown in Chapter 11, the customers' emotional response is critical for predicting key advertising success metrics, including sales growth, purchase intent, brand recall, and likelihood of sharing. Without the help of this technology, it's hard to predict the performance of an ad, especially considering that the same advertisement can work for one set of customers but not for another.

When it comes to customer acquisition, AI-based tools are used by the sales teams as well. In many instances, AI comes integrated with the CRM systems (an example of that is Salesforce Einstein which integrates AI technology with Salesforce's Software-as-a-Service (SaaS) CRM system) and provides functionality such as conversational assistants and next best action recommendations. When AI is embedded in the customer data platform (CDP), it allows organizations to understand where in the sales cycle the customer is at and the things that the customers are most interested in through the data that customers produce. This is then used to present customers with more relevant content and offers. The technology also enables the organization to direct salespeople to prospects that are more likely to convert by doing forecasting and lead opportunity scoring.

AI Use in Customer Relationship Building and Retention

Retaining a customer typically costs several times less than acquiring a new one and losing a customer due to bad experience could also have more repercussions with negative word of mouth. So naturally, this is another key area where AI could make an impact.

As we have said earlier in this book, our research found that, of the traditional touchpoints, Customer service had the biggest impact on Emotional attachment, with the latter being the biggest driver of value for organizations. This is also where we have seen a good AI solution.

Many business people perceive the contact center as a cost to the business, but if it's managed right, it could also be a big driver of value and a competitive differentiator. I remember how 10 to 15 years ago most contact centers were either in or moving to India to save costs but that didn't prove to be much beneficial for organizations and that trend seems reversed now. I remember when working with a telecom in the Middle East how a senior executive was sacked because he was the one pushing to move the contact center to India; he chose a partner there but the whole thing turned out to be a disaster. On the other hand, I have been behind the scenes of many contact centers in the United Kingdom and the United States where the level of service was really amazing because the agents were trained really well and were being looked after. It was those interactions that reaffirmed the customer's perception, built esteem of the organization, and contributed to the feeling of a relationship.

The key to turning the contact center from cost to the business to a value driver is training and continuous coaching (ah and one more thing, stop being obsessed with "average hand time"). As we have said before, "people don't know what they don't know." Some people are more natural at this; some people will be better at certain types of interactions or interacting with certain types of customers, while others would excel in different settings. So coaching is very important.

Yet, while every time you contact an organization they say that the "call is being recorded for quality purposes," only a fraction of those will actually be reviewed by someone trying to assess the quality of the interaction and provide coaching to staff members. The other thing that I get surprised by every time that I visit a call center is that hardly ever can you find a running statistic for the reasons of contact, the satisfaction with those, retention rates, and so on. This kind of call reason tracking mechanism is very important when it comes to identifying reasons for unwanted calls that don't provide value for customers and are just a cost to the organization and thus can be eliminated by identifying the root-cause driver and applying a design intervention. When it comes to the quality control of calls, you won't be surprised to learn that human evaluations of the agent's handling of customer interactions and their soft skills are subject to unconscious biases and are rated inconsistently. A research was conducted on a same set of customer calls where agents were rated on a set of key soft-skills such as "build rapport," "demonstrate ownership," and "listen actively" on one side by human listeners and on another by an AI-powered behavioral model rating. The results showed large scoring variances and inconsistencies when scored by humans, while the NICE ENLIGHTEN behavior analysis model showed no variance in the evaluation of soft-skill behaviors. [3]

Just like all roads lead to Rome, through various channels, we came across the NICE ENLIGHTEN AI framework for real-time analytics that is used in call centers (including the call center of a leading U.S. bank, which told us about the wonderful things it does). Their framework "allows agents to proactively self-correct during a customer interaction to drive a positive outcome, while monitoring customer behaviors for indications of complaints or fraudster profiles."

Before we talk more about it let's take a step back and explain some of the fundamentals of the analysis in the contact center settings. Remember in Chapter 11 we spoke about the work of professor Paul Watzlawick, who had found that when partner relationships were on the verge of collapse it was not what was said (i.e., the communication) but rather how it was said (i.e., the metacommunication) that was causing the breakdown. Similarly, when an AI is analyzing the communication it looks not just at what is said, but how it's said and what emotions are conveyed. In the context of AI analytics, this is referred to as sentiment analysis. It could be done on any data stored as voice (calls) or text (chats, e-mails, social media posts, etc.). Sentiment analysis then employs models looking to find positive or negative words and phrases and the AI machine learning (ML) algorithm is trained through millions of interactions to predict the outcome of the interaction. Training the model could be based initially on human scoring of these interactions and would be made much more powerful with the addition of actual data on repeat contacts, customer satisfaction, likelihood to recommend scores, and actual customer churn data.

Another very interesting thing in the NICE-sponsored *AI-Enabled Contact Center Analytics for Dummies*® e-book is that sentiment models observe that phrases occurring toward the end of an interaction have a stronger prediction of outcome than those spoken earlier in the call. Studies show that the latter portion of an interaction drives customers' reported satisfaction more heavily than the former. [4]

Remember when we spoke about Kahnemann's peak–end rule! This is another evidence of how powerful it is. The endings are very important and organizations should be deliberate about the design of the end of customer interactions.

So through AI predictive analytics an organization can capture the customer sentiment and identify the agent behaviors that are driving customer satisfaction. The AI algorithm works to analyze the file recording measuring the emotional components of each call—empathy, cross talk (i.e., how much employees talk over the customer), how much dead-air there was, and so on. Based on this the model assigns a sentiment score to each call (i.e., like customer satisfaction). Sentiment analysis is measured on every single call and is objective, as no humans are involved and it's the same algorithm assessing all calls. On the next day, the organization will get the sentiment analysis of what the interactions looked like from an organizational level down to an individual level.

The model will also allow for better one-to-one coaching and agent assessment across key behaviors proven to drive customer satisfaction. This allows managers to coach more efficiently, using the system to direct them on what to coach as opposed to randomly listening to calls and trying to find ones that would meet what they want to coach.

Interestingly, those proven behaviors are almost identical to the emotions that were most common in our Emotional attachment grouping (Table 2.3) and professor Harry Reis's principles for healthy partner relationships, i.e. *understanding, validation* (making the partner feel respected and valued, which support the feeling of belonging and security), and *caring.* Among the key agent behaviors in the NICE ENLIGHTEN model are things like "actively listening" (i.e., understanding); "empathizing," that is, showing that you have actively listened and understood not just the customer issue but also the emotional pain that it inflicted on the customer; "showing respect"; and "acknowledge loyalty," with the latter being at the end of the list (an important part of the "ending ceremony"). This is a confirmation by the AI-powered research on something we said earlier in the book. In Chapter 5, we discussed how important it is from a psychological perspective to show that you "know" the customer and acknowledge the relationship. By monitoring for the key agent behaviors the AI model can then assess the extent to which agents posed the right questions to understand the issue, actively listened to what the customer said, and managed to establish a personal connection. Depending on the setup, the algorithm could also provide real-time suggestions (coaching advice) and even kudos for good performance to call center agents.

Then it gets even more interesting. We spoke earlier in the book about how important personalization is, yet there are hardly any companies out there that route customers to the right agents based on the customer's unique needs and personality. How many times did you wish you could speak to the same agent you spoke to earlier but that wasn't possible? Or that you get to an agent that you can enjoy conversing with? One more advanced U.K.-based mortgage company was teaching their agents about listening for clues to the customer's personality type. They had established four customer personas: a "controller," a "thinker," a "feeler," and an "entertainer" and had trained their agents to adjust the balance between details and speed of the interaction according to which customer type they were speaking to. But what if instead customers were routed to the agent type that they are most likely to build rapport with? Well, now you can with predictive behavioral routing (PBR) solutions. "PBR uses data on the customer's personality, behavioral characteristics, and communication preferences gathered from previous interactions to predict intelligently the best agent to handle the customer's call, and then route the call to that agent."

I've always been a believer that the right way of doing business is also more cost effective. You can also save costs by increasing the rate of first contact resolution by analyzing the root-cause problem for the customer contact, identifying broken processes, or just getting the necessary information ("knowledge articles") in front of the agent to resolve the customer issue. Agents typically spend a lot of time searching for information but now with the advancement of natural language processing (NLP), those articles could appear automatically to agents and can later be further assessed as to how helpful they are or which is the right article to show as the algorithm keeps learning all the time.

Working with a large insurance company in the United Kingdom we once learned that agents were saying to customers that they *should* get their documents in five days. This resulted in a 75 percent call back rate with customers calling on the fourth day and saying "Am I getting the documents?" The agents had changed just one word from the script. According to the script, agents were to say "you will get your documents…," but the agents were using "should" because they didn't want to lie to customers knowing that the postal services were not always the most reliable. The company advised agents to start using "will" again but this time they increased the timeline to seven business days. Within two weeks the percentage of repeat calls dropped to 6 percent, eliminating hundreds of thousands of unwanted calls. Similarly, working with a water utility company in the United Kingdom, we learned that resending a crew to a customer location was costing them £60 to £70 ($80 to $95) and a major contributor to that was the agent not capturing or entering correctly the real customer issue. We believe that these types of cost drivers would be more easily identified with the help of AI and it could lead to some cost savings in addition to customer retention benefits.

Not only that but it could improve sales effectiveness as well by offering relevant promotions or doing in-call prompts to agents to listen more, change their tone, ask appropriate questions, and so on.

A user of this system also said that among the possibilities the system offers is the ability to get the internal data and analytics gurus to write queries into those text interactions and to start pulling out themes. For example, "What are our customers saying about our newly released product?" Then as the company starts making decisions on what improvements to make next, they will have the data to say "hey this is an issue but in only 3 percent of the interactions whereas this is an issue in 12 percent of the interactions." They can measure why customers are contacting them and what they are contacting them for, what isn't an issue only in the contact center, what is happening in digital interactions, in social media, and so on.

The aforementioned is of course just one of the many AI tools out there. The leading application of AI when it comes to customer service is in the use of chatbots. While those were dreaded interactions in the early days, chatbots are now coming of age. After all, that's why it's called ML, isn't it! A must-do in the use of chatbots for me is to always remember to allow for a human to take over the conversation if the customer can't resolve its issue through the chatbot. Chatbots are good to solve a bunch of transactional problems. They can speed up finding relevant information, take care of general customer service requests such as cancellations (some companies have buried that option so much that one has to use the AI chatbot), and other minor issues. However, probably many of you have been locked in a closed loop with a chatbot where after several tries you still get to the same place but your problem is still not resolved and there is no option to escalate the issue to a human. Organizations should use chatbots to automate straightforward transactions and use the savings to redirect employees to more value-added activities, either handling more complex interactions, acting more as advisors to customers, or doing more analytical work on the data from the interactions to drive further improvements and eliminate unnecessary causes for contacts. Chatbots, now evolving to conversational AI, should be seen not so much as a replacement for the human workforce but as a supplement, allowing them to be more efficient or to be deployed to more value-adding activities.

Given all the applications of AI we discussed earlier, it should come as no surprise to learn from the Aberdeen report "The Intelligent Contact Center" (June 2020) that firms using AI enjoy 3.5× greater annual improvement in customer satisfaction, 8× greater annual decrease in customer effort rates, and 3.3× greater annual improvement in client retention rates (10.5 vs. 3.2 percent) compared to nonusers. This leads to a 6.5 percent year-on-year (YoY) increase in annual revenue for AI users compared to the 2.9 percent worsening by nonusers. This means a quite significant 9.4 percent gap in revenue growth between users and nonusers of AI. [5]

This shows that AI, the mix of data and technology, could have a substantial impact on an organization's performance. However, it is not a panacea to all problems and a sure recipe for success.

Many companies have jumped on the big data–ML bandwagon but there are a few shortcomings to their strategy being solely based on big data. For once, in pursuing predictive ability through AI analysis of big data they risk sacrificing the interpretability of the results, understanding the why behind the results, or what to do on the back of it.

The next important thing is what data organizations use to run their analysis. The reality is that most organizations turn to their CRM (customer relationship management) systems, loyalty programs, or past purchases for their data needs. While undoubtedly this will give them a big data pool, what it means is that the organization will rely on historical, internal data at the expense of forward-looking insights into changing customer preferences and unmet needs. The data in the CRM system will also be biased toward existing customers, while the audience with the biggest growth potential may lie elsewhere with different needs and emotional drivers. So strategies built solely on the basis of internal CRM data may end up being too inward- and backward-looking.

In fact, Forrester did an experiment, running regression analysis on the type of data that is typically stored in a CRM system. They found

that the frequency with which consumers interact with the brand, the length of time the consumer has subscribed to the brand, and the frequency with which consumers purchase from the brand are not statistically relevant indicators of brand loyalty, brand advocacy, or the intent to continue subscribing. [6]

Therefore, as Forrester concluded, "just because the data is plentiful it doesn't mean it's all-powerful." What organizations need to do instead is combine big data with what is referred to as small data. That means combining the power of AI-based predictive analytics with strategic customer surveys, looking to find the key value drivers (rational, emotional, and subconscious), and in-depth customer interviews, which provide more context into the perceived motivators or barriers to adopting the products and services of an organization (answering the question why one would buy from the organization while another one won't).

Jason Ten-Pow, author of *UNBREAKABLE: A Proven Process for Building Unbreakable Relationships With Customers* (CX Publishing House Incorporated 2021) and CEO of CX consulting firm ONR, shares the same opinion. He and his team had done analysis using internally available data about customer behavior on an organization's website (i.e., number of page visits, number of clicks, length of stay, etc.) and found that the behavior has almost no impact on whether or not they are satisfied with that experience but the emotion has enormous impact. "When you look at how they felt about for example navigating the website, was it frustrating or not, that alone has a 50 percent impact on whether or not they would be satisfied with the website," he says. "Small data is great for digging into why. Big data—helps you understand what to gig into. It'll pinpoint where the problem is. The problem with big data is in its name itself—it's big, it's unmanageable," he goes on to add. [7]

In summary, we would see more and more organizations tapping into the power of AI to optimize their customer acquisition strategies and improve customer relationship building and retention. In the sales funnel stages, AI can help develop better customer profiling, targeting, and personalization mechanisms to increase conversions and improve marketing efficiency. AI could certainly be of good use when it comes to improving interactions with existing customers. We provided evidence of the successful application in the call center environment and earlier in the book we discussed how AI-powered facial emotion recognition could be used for insights into the digital experience and how Walmart may use it in the physical retail environment. These are just some of the possibilities. We provided some examples of AI use cases that make a meaningful impact on customer interactions but there are, of course, other use cases and a host of AI solutions that could be used in product development, production, malfunction detection, and so on.

Another useful application of AI-based solutions would be in the analysis of big masses of data. Here, however, research suggests that organizations shouldn't solely rely on big data but also combine it with the so-called small data, that is, customer surveys looking to find the rational, emotional, and subconscious drivers of customer behavior and in-depth interviews to provide more context for those drivers (i.e., explain the why).

As you can imagine, this is not something that many organizations do and this takes us to the final chapter of the book, where will discuss how the future of customer experience management lies in creating a fusion between data, technology, behavioral science, and the knowledge of what it takes to manage customer experience inside the organization.

Practitioner Tips From This Chapter

How to make the best of the new AI tools to drive business growth?

- Think about your business problems and data needs. Where could data and insights help you the most? How could you collect and analyze that data?
- If your focus is on customer acquisition, AI can help profile your customer base and find the behavioral patterns that lead to conversions. AI-powered facial emotion recognition applications can also be used to gauge consumer reactions to your marketing materials. AI can also help with better targeting and personalized content. Beware that you don't solely focus on the more easily measurable and with immediate impact lower-funnel activities (i.e., sales and discount offers) but you also aim to build the brand (i.e., upper-funnel activities) and develop an emotional attachment with customers (e.g., what we discussed in Chapter 11).
- If your focus is on customer relationship building and retention, the advancement of NLP capabilities means that AI can be used to analyze voice and text interactions, mine the data, drive insights, and improve the coaching mechanism.
- AI can also help with the analysis of big masses of data. However, there should also be a note of caution with all this. Relying on historical, internal data may be at the expense of forward-looking insights into changing customer preferences and unmet needs. Then there is the problem of interpretability of the results and understanding the why behind customer behavior. Therefore, practitioners should mix the use of AI and big data predictive analytics with small data insights (i.e., customer surveys, in-depth interviews, etc.).

CHAPTER 14

The Rise of Customer Science Teams

Behind every business problem to be solved, there is a human problem to be solved.

—Cerita Bethea

Just as I was writing some of the above lines I came across the news in a *Wall Street Journal* article that McDonald's had named its first global chief customer officer (CCO), who will lead a new customer-experience team. This by itself is not news as it comes exactly a decade after Paul Hagan's HBR article "The Rise of the Chief Customer Officer," which highlights how more and more organizations are appointing a senior executive to be responsible for the customer experience and sit on the board of directors.

What made an impression on me is the description of his job role and function, that is: "The team will combine operations in data analytics, digital customer engagement, marketing, restaurant development and restaurant solutions, a segment that includes areas such as drive-through services and how food is cooked." The newly appointed CCO, Manu Steijaert, who has been with McDonald's for more than two decades, then goes on to say, "we have reached a pivotal moment when technology and data have begun to shape nearly every facet of the customer experience." [1]

What this shows to me is that the future of customer experience is now. It is a blend of data and technology, a blend between the digital and physical customer experience, and requires a cross-silo approach. Just think about how many different traditional departments the CX function has to collaborate with (not step on): IT, customer insights (research), digital, marketing, retail, business development, product development, and so on.

The news for this appointment comes about a year after Colin Shaw, the founder, and CEO of Beyond Philosophy, who has always had an eye and a good hunch about what the future holds, sent me an e-mail about Amazon Science. Amazon Science's LinkedIn page tagline says "customer-obsessed science." The page says, "Amazon fundamentally believes that scientific innovation is essential to being the most customer-centric company in the world." [2] It goes on to mention the importance of "artificial intelligence" and "engage with the academic community."

These are our beliefs as well. Throughout this book, we have referenced the work of many academics which provide scientific breakthroughs in our understanding of how the human mind works, what creates or breaks relationships, what creates emotions, how emotions affect our perception of advertising, and many more. We have also referenced the work of many behavioral scientists and some behavioral science principles, for example, "the peak–end rule," "the mere-exposure effect," "social proof," "the Benjamin Franklin effect." and so on. The field of behavioral science is unique and fascinating on its own as it combines the disciplines of psychology, economics, and neuroscience. It is therefore our belief that customer experience teams need to adopt science as their gospel, have knowledge of and use behavioral science in the design of products, services, and the customer experience. The CX teams also need to keep in touch with the academic community to stay on top of the latest developments in customer science.

Just like behavioral science combines the fields of psychology, economics, and neuroscience, the customer experience teams of the future need to combine data and technology, behavioral science, and customer experience management skills to drive organic, customer-centered growth of the organization.

The foundation for this customer-driven growth and innovation should be based on data and insights. As discussed in the previous chapter, an organization should use AI predictive analytics, customer value driver research, and in-depth customer interviews in conjunction to be able to really understand the conscious and unconscious drivers of customer behavior, the behavioral science principles in play, and the intrinsic motivators and perceived barriers that make one customer opt in for the organization's products and services while another one opts out. This will move organizations from being mostly reactive in their customer experience efforts to being more proactive. Today, most organizations would react to the customer showing signs of intent to leave and then offer incentives to keep the customer. Having conducted hundreds of interviews with lost customers, we know that most often than not, this is too little, too late as the customer had already made their mind, and offering a monetary incentive is only adding to the insult, which has typically been on an emotional basis (i.e., the customer not feeling appreciated, respected, understood, cared for, or having lost trust in the organization).

In the future, firms could be deploying predictive analytics, scanning a large data pool of interactions, and using AI to find the early signs of a customer moving on a path to churn and then deploy less costly, more behaviorally infused nudges, to change the future relationship prospects. For example, if AI speech analytics are used in the contact center, the tool may find that when the customer raises his/her voice at the end of an interaction to a certain level (perhaps to the level of shouting), the data from past interactions may suggest that there is a high probability that this customer then leaves within X months and so automatically flag this customer to the retention team. For example, working with an electricity provider in a deregulated U.S. market, we found that many of their churned customers had left because their contract had expired and for some reason or another they had missed or failed to act on the renewal communications and thus they were put on "default," higher-priced plans. Once those customers started to see the higher bills, they started to shop around, and then in many instances, it was too late for the organization to offer them good deals as the "genie had left the bottle" and they had chosen the deal from another energy company. With AI onboard, the AI could have analyzed the customer usage and offered an appropriate plan or simply put customers on a plan that best suits their usage patterns.

As we said, the future is now and this is exactly what Symend does. They combine data with AI analytics and use behavioral science in the design of interventions to retain customers and change the projective nature of their relationship with the organization.

Symend is a Canadian startup that helps companies such as financial institutions, telecoms, and utilities identify and assist customers struggling to pay bills. The Covid-19 pandemic led to a sharp increase in customers falling behind on bill payments. While most service providers' main strategy in such circumstances has been to offer customers deferral periods in order to avoid defaults, Symend takes a different, more behavioral science-led approach. They have found that when customers default, typically they default on average of three bills (mostly down on loan, mortgage/rent, or credit card payments) and therefore providing a deferral period "can provide a false sense of financial security for customers," says Hanif Joshaghani, the company's CEO and cofounder. [3] So they try to identify customers at risk early on and use behavioral nudges to change their behavior and suggest payment alternatives to prevent them from defaulting altogether.

How do they use data science and behavior science to create a personalized approach to each customer? A TechCrunch article by Ingrid Lunden sheds some light on.

First, Symend looks at the data available in their client's internal systems and combines that with third-party data to find key patterns in customer profiles and behavior that lead to defaulting and churn. They do that using behaviorally informed models. Combining insights from customer interactions with historical data on actions taken, their AI/ML model helps "discover underlying psychological and behavioral traits to determine which engagement strategies will positively shape behavior." In other words, they are personalizing their interventions according to the profile and behavior of each individual customer. But that's not all. They monitor customer's reaction to their nudges using NLP models to "automatically categorize sentiment based on provided responses to communications and within self-serve tools" and are then able to further iterate their nudges to change the customer behavior.

The focus of all this is to engage customers in empathic communication and provide customers with a positive experience in an otherwise stressful situation. As we've said before, the right way of doing business is also more cost effective. So by providing customers with more flexible payment options using digital self-serve channels, they are not only alleviating pressure from the already overwhelmed and stretched call centers in Covid-19 times but also helping them retain customers by preventing defaults and increasing customer satisfaction.

The Symend example comes to illustrate how organizations could combine the use of data, AI analytics, and digital tools all in one cohesive customer experience and business strategy that drives growth and even reduces costs. In the future, CX leaders should focus on designing a cohesive insights system, one that relies on data and science, uses quantitative and qualitative methods to diagnose what behavioral bottlenecks may be impacting the customer's perceptions and behavior. They can then use behavioral science in the design of interventions that address the diagnosed problems. Equipped with new analysis methods, they can uncover unexpected insights into how different people and groups respond to different treatments and scale personalized strategies.

This obviously requires CX leaders to be supported by a team. It'll be data scientists that write the algorithms for ML and behavioral scientists that design nudges and interventions. As we have said before, the customer experience function needs not to be a vertical and create its own silo, but to be a horizontal just as data will be spanning across finance, operations, customer service, sales, product performance, and so on. So CX leaders need to interact with the various business unit leaders to better understand how data and customer knowledge can help them drive the organization's strategy and goals.

The important lessons of this book are to always start with the customer's needs first. Find the real drivers of their behavior, which are often emotional and subconscious. Then design interventions or changes to the experience that drive the desired customer behavior. Oftentimes what affects the customer's attitude the most has little to do with technology so it's important to start with the customer and business problem first and then see where, how, and what technology can make the experience better and drive emotional attachment.

Throughout this book, we have provided overwhelming evidence about how emotions are key drivers of customer behavior and brought in academic research that helps explain why emotions are so important in the experience and yet customers themselves are not aware of that. The latter probably explains why emotions are not featuring so much on business radars and that leads to big missed opportunities for businesses.

Given the enormous opportunity to create an emotional attachment with customers, differentiate, and drive organic growth, organizations should pursue a deliberate approach to evoking the emotions that drive the most value for them. This strategy should be based on data and science, rather than guesswork. New technologies and digital solutions should also be adopted with that goal in mind. Organizations need to integrate data with behavioral science to ask the right questions and find the behavior bottlenecks right at the onset, rather than "stacking hay to search for a needle." AI can help analyze the masses of data and provide insights at a granular level while also being ethical in the use of anonymized customer data. Behavioral science can then help interpret that data and devise interventions. Customer experience management science can help drive these capabilities and actions forward to achieve customer-driven growth. The future of nurturing and managing customer relations therein lies in creating a fusion between data and technology, behavioral science, and customer experience expertise to drive emotional attachment with customers and growth.

Practitioner Tips From This Chapter

How to create organizational capabilities for sustainable customer experience improvement and organizational growth?

- Establish a customer science team with capabilities to combine the use of data science, technology, and behavioral science in the design of the customer experience.
- Find the drivers of customer behavior (conscious and unconscious).
- Undoubtedly, emotions will play a role in your experience and will be affecting customer behavior to various extents, so don't leave the emotional experience to chance. Approach creating an emotional attachment with customers as a science and a strategy.

References

Introduction

1. Turvill, W. August 01, 2016. "Trinity Mirror Boss: New Day Failed Because Consumers Didn't Want What They Said They Wanted." *CITYA.M.com*. www.cityam.com/trinity-mirror-boss-new-day-newspaper-failed-because/
2. Elliott, S. February 22, 2009. "Tropicana Discovers Some Buyers Are Passionate About Packaging." *The New York Times*. www.nytimes.com/2009/02/23/business/media/23adcol.html?pagewanted=all
3. Grobart, S. September 16, 2016. "How Chase Made the Perfect High for Credit Card Junkies." *Bloomberg*. www.bloomberg.com/news/features/2016-09-22/how-chase-made-the-perfect-high-for-credit-card-junkies
4. "The Link Between W_eight and Importance." *PsychologicalScience.org*. August 31, 2009. www.psychologicalscience.org/news/releases/the-link-between-weight-and-importance.html
5. Grobart, S. September 16, 2016. "How Chase Made the Perfect High for Credit Card Junkies." Bloomberg. www.bloomberg.com/news/features/2016-09-22/how-chase-made-the-perfect-high-for-credit-card-junkies
6. Wilson, L. December 03, 2020. "UK Challenger Banks: Who's Winning the Race?" *Beauhurst*. www.beauhurst.com/blog/uk-challenger-banks/
7. ZoBell, S. March 13, 2018. "Why Digital Transformations Fail: Closing The $900 Billion Hole In Enterprise Strategy." *Forbes*. www.forbes.com/sites/forbestechcouncil/2018/03/13/why-digital-transformations-fail-closing-the-900-billion-hole-in-enterprise-strategy/?sh=7dfcc33d7b8b

Chapter 1

1. Altman, L. n.d. "How Emotion Shapes Decision Making." *Intentional Communication Consultants*. www.intentionalcommunication.com/how-emotion-shapes-decision-making/ (accessed March 18, 2021).
2. Altman. n.d. "How Emotion Shapes Decision Making." *Intentional Communication Consultants*. www.intentionalcommunication.com/how-emotion-shapes-decision-making/ (accessed March 18, 2021).
3. Barrett, A. March 2017. "Age Diversity Within Boards of Directors of the S&P 500 Companies, IRRC Institute." *KPMG*. https://assets.kpmg/content/dam/kpmg/jm/pdf/FINAL-Age-Diversity-Study-March-2017.pdf
4. Author interview with Ten-Pow, J. June 02, 2021.

Chapter 2

1. Dixon, M., K. Freeman, and N. Toman. July–August 2010. "Stop Trying to Delight Your Customers." *HBR.* https://hbr.org/2010/07/stop-trying-to-delight-your-customers

2. Hagen, P. February 15, 2012. "Conversations With Customer Experience Leaders: Maersk Line's Jesper Engelbrecht Thomsen." *Forrester.* www.forrester.com/report/Conversations+With+Customer+Experience+Leaders+Maersk+Lines+Jesper+Engelbrecht+Thomsen/-/E-RES60393

3. Leiblum, S.R., E. Schnall, M. Seehuus, and A. DeMaria. 2008. "To BATHE or Not to BATHE: Patient Satisfaction With Visits to Their Family Physician." *Fam Med* 40, no. 6, pp. 407–411. https://www.researchgate.net/publication/23239833_To_BATHE_or_not_to_BATHE_Patient_satisfaction_with_visits_to_their_family_physician

4. Pace, E.J., N.J. Somerville, C. Enyioha, J.P. Allen, L.C. Lemon, and C.W. Allen. 2017. "Effects of a Brief Psychosocial Intervention on Inpatient Satisfaction: A Randomized Controlled Trial." *Fam Med* 49, no. 9, pp. 675–678. https://fammedarchives.blob.core.windows.net/imagesandpdfs/pdfs/FamilyMedicineVol49Issue9Pace675.pdf

5. Leiblum, S.R., E. Schnall, M. Seehuus, and A. DeMaria. 2008. "To BATHE or Not to BATHE: Patient Satisfaction With Visits to Their Family Physician." Fam Med 40, no. 6, pp. 407–411. https://www.researchgate.net/publication/23239833_To_BATHE_or_not_to_BATHE_Patient_satisfaction_with_visits_to_their_family_physician

6. DeMaria, S., A. DeMaria, M. Weiner, and G. Silvay. 2010. "Use of the BATHE Method to Increase Satisfaction Amongst Patients Undergoing Cardiac and Major Vascular Operations." *Cleve Clin J Med* 77(Electronic Suppl 1), pp. eS25–eS25. https://www.ccjm.org/content/ccjom/77/3_esuppl_1/eS25.full.pdf

7. DeMaria, S., A. DeMaria, G. Silvay, and B. Flynn. 2011. "Use of the BATHE Method in the Preanesthetic Clinic Visit." *Anesth Analg* 113, no. 5, pp. 1020–1026. doi: 10.1213/ANE.0b013e318229497b. https://www.researchgate.net/publication/51593878_Use_of_the_BATHE_Method_in_the_Preanesthetic_Clinic_Visit

8. Kim, J., Y.N. Park, E.W. Park, Y.S. Cheong, and E.Y. Choi. 2012. "Effects of BATHE Interview Protocol on Patient Satisfaction." *Korean J Fam Med* 33, no. 6, pp. 366–371. https://www.researchgate.net/publication/233984881_Effects_of_BATHE_Interview_Protocol_on_Patient_Satisfaction

9. Pace, E.J., N.J. Somerville, C. Enyioha, J.P. Allen, L.C. Lemon, and C.W. Allen. 2017. "Effects of a Brief Psychosocial Intervention on Inpatient Satisfaction: A Randomized Controlled Trial." Fam Med 49, no. 9, pp. 675–678. https://fammedarchives.blob.core.windows.net/imagesandpdfs/pdfs/FamilyMedicineVol49Issue9Pace675.pdf

10. HCAHPS Fact Sheet. June 2015. "Centers for Medicare & Medicaid Services (CMS)." Baltimore, MD USA. www.hcahpsonline.org/ Facts.aspx (accessed August 26, 2016).

Chapter 3

1. Kershner, K. n.d. "What's the Baader-Meinhof Phenomenon?" *howstuffworks. com*, updated August 10, 2021 https://science.howstuffworks.com/life/ inside-the-mind/human-brain/baader-meinhof-phenomenon.htm

2. Reis, H.T. 2014. "Responsiveness: Affective Interdependence in Close Relationships." In M. Mikulincer and P.R. Shaver (eds.), "The Herzliya Series on Personality and Social Psychology. Mechanisms of Social Connection: From Brain to Group." *American Psychological Association*, pp. 255–271. https://doi.org/10.1037/14250-015

3. Heath, C., and D. Heath. 2017. "The Power of Moments: Why Certain Experiences Have Extraordinary Impact." *Simon & Schuster*. https:// www.amazon.com/Power-Moments-Certain-Experiences-Extraordinary/ dp/1501147765

4. *Newswire*. September 27, 2018. "New Retail Study Shows Marketers Under-Leverage Emotional Connection." www.prnewswire.com/news-releases/new-retail-study-shows-marketers-under-leverage-emotional-connection-300720049.html

5. "Leveraging the Value of Emotional Connection for Retailers." *Motista.com*. www.motista.com/resource/emotions-best-predict-growth-retailers

6. Magids, S., A. Zorfas, and D. Leemon. November 2015. "The New Science of Customer Emotions: A Better Way to Drive Growth and Profitability." *Harvard Business Review*. https://hbr.org/2015/11/the-new-science-of-customer-emotions

7. *Motista.com*. April 2021. "Ranking Emotional Connection: A look at 50 of the Top U.S. Brands." www.motista.com/system/files/50%20Top%20 Brands_2.pdf

8. Jones, K. December 07, 2020. "Pandemic Proof: The Most Loved Brands of COVID-19." *Visual Capitalist*. www.visualcapitalist.com/pandemic-proof-the-most-loved-brands-of-covid-19/

9. MBLM—Brand Intimacy COVID Study. April 2021. http://content.mblm. com/bis-covid-report

10. MBLM website. April 202. https://mblm.com/lab/resources/methodology/

11. *Choicehacking*. 2021. "How to Use Behavioral Science to Create a Positive Emotional Experience." https://choicehacking.com/2021/03/07/behavioral-science-emotional-experience/?fbclid=IwAR0A1u6C2GN2bNgMAFIqjzR8 MeZGwfPgevl62k_VjNXfAt_24Jtf9zAPL7Q (accessed March 18, 2021).

Forrester Research, Inc. June 2019. "How Customers Think, Feel, And Act: The Paradigm Of Business Outcomes." https://cloud.kapostcontent.net/pub/ d2a85d5e-c053-4bfc-ae8d-f1a9c0b2af31/whitepaper-how-customers-think-feel- and-act-the-paradigm-of-business-outcomes?kui=MtTZamfFfmzvSS4fnSaD4Q

Chapter 4

1. Kahneman, D. n.d. "The Riddle of Experience vs Memory." *TED Talk.* www.ted.com/talks/daniel_kahneman_the_riddle_of_experience_vs_ memory?language=en (accessed March 18, 2021).
2. Reisberg, D., and P. Hertel. 2004. "Memory and Emotion." *Oxford University Press,* p.13. https://books.google.bg/books?hl=en&lr=&id=TemvZpgA6uoC&oi= fnd&pg=PR13&dq=emotions+influence+memory+retention+ and+recall&ots=wXrxDMLCoH&sig=CkAw8gwYNfnQ07S_W90rkIXq MGI&redir_esc=y#v=onepage&q=emotions%20influence%20memory %20retention%20and%20recall&f=false
3. Zimmer, C. May 10, 2005. "Scientist at Work: Michael Gazzaniga; A Career Spent Learning How the Mind Emerges From the Brain." *The New York Times.* www.nytimes.com/2005/05/10/science/a-career-spent-learning-how- the-mind-emerges-from-the-brain.html
4. Mahoney, M. January 13, 2003. "The Subconscious Mind of the Consumer (And How To Reach It)." *Harvard Business School.* https://hbswk.hbs.edu/ item/the-subconscious-mind-of-the-consumer-and-how-to-reach-it
5. North, A.C., D.J. Hargreaves, and J. McKendrick. 1999. "The Influence of In-Store Music on Wine Selections." *Journal of Applied Psychology* 84, no. 2, pp. 271–276. https://doi.org/10.1037/0021-9010.84.2.271
6. Shiv, B., and A. Fedorikhin. December 1999. "Heart and Mind in Conflict: The Interplay of Affect and Cognition in Consumer Decision Making." *Journal of Consumer Research* 26, no. 3, pp. 278–292. https://www.researchgate.net/ publication/24099033_Heart_and_Mind_in_Conflict_The_Interplay_of_ Affect_and_Cognition_in_Consumer_Decision_Making
7. Dijksterhuis, A. October 2009. "The Beautiful Powers of Unconscious Thought." *American Psychological Association, Science Briefs.* www.apa.org/ science/about/psa/2009/10/sci-brief

Chapter 5

1. "Transforming healthcare for children and their families: Doug Dietz at TEDxSanJoseCA." 2012. www.youtube.com/watch?v=jajduxPD6H4
2. *IDEOU.* n.d. "From Design Thinking to Creative Confidence." www.ideou .com/blogs/inspiration/from-design-thinking-to-creative-confidence

3. Lee J. n.d. "Design for All 5 Senses." *TED Talks*. www.youtube.com/watch?v=N6wjC0sxD2o&t=1s

4. Kelley, T., and D. Kelley. 2013. *Creative Confidence: Unleashing the Creative Potential Within Us All*. Crown Business. https://www.amazon.com/Creative-Confidence-Unleashing-Potential-Within/dp/038534936X

5. Pine, B.J., II, and J.H. Gilmore. July–August 1998. "Welcome to the Experience Economy." *HBR*. https://hbr.org/1998/07/welcome-to-the-experience-economy

6. Bradley, D. November 21, 2013. "'AmEx' Asks Customers to Embrace 'member since' Date." *PR week*. www.prweek.com/article/1274051/amex-asks-customers-embrace-member-since-date

7. RedFlagDeals forum. n.d. "American Express Member Since." https://forums.redflagdeals.com/american-express-member-since-2257185/

8. *Twice.com*. January 22, 2018. "Why Customer Service Reps Are Really In The Baggage Handling Business." www.twice.com/blog/customer-service-rep-as-baggage-handler-ceb

9. Heath, C., and D. Heath. 2017. "The Power of Moments: Why Certain Experiences Have Extraordinary Impact." *Simon & Schuster*, p. 239. https://www.amazon.com/Power-Moments-Certain-Experiences-Extraordinary/dp/1501147765

10. Duhigg, C. 2012. "The Power of Habit: Why We Do What We Do in Life and Business." *Random House*, p. 211. https://www.amazon.com/Power-Habit-What-Life-Business/dp/081298160X

11. Huo, Y.H., and K.R. Binning. 2008. "Why the Psychological Experience of Respect Matters in Group Life: An Integrative Account." *Social and Personality Psychology Compass* 2. 10.1111/j.1751-9004.2008.00129.x. https://www.researchgate.net/publication/227545448_Why_the_Psychological_Experience_of_Respect_Matters_in_Group_Life_An_Integrative_Account

12. Google/Ipsos. 2019. U.S., "Shopping Tracker," online survey, n=2,551 shoppers who return to a retailer site, Q3 2019. https://www.thinkwithgoogle.com/consumer-insights/consumer-trends/you-dont-just-need-personalization-you-need-the-right-personalization/

13. Google/BCG. 2019. U.S., "Business Impact of Personalization in Retail" study and customer survey, n=3,144. https://www.thinkwithgoogle.com/consumer-insights/consumer-trends/you-dont-just-need-personalization-you-need-the-right-personalization/

14. *Bain*. March 11, 2021. Webinar: "Delivering Authentic and Individualized Experiences to Every Customer." www.bain.com/insights/delivering-authentic-and-individualized-experiences-to-every-customer-webinar/

15. Hill, K. February 16, 2012. "How Target Figured Out A Teen Girl Was Pregnant Before Her Father." *Forbes*. www.forbes.com/sites/kashmirhill/2012/02/16/how-target-figured-out-a-teen-girl-was-pregnant-before-her-father-did/?sh=63aab15a6668

16. *UX Collective.* February 24, 2021. "The Barnum Effect and the Sweet Nothings of Astrology." https://uxdesign.cc/the-barnum-effect-and-the-sweet-nothings-of-astrology-c363e1f3754d

17. Norman, D. 2002. "Emotion & Design: Attractive Things Work Better." *Interactions Magazine* 9, pp. 36–42. 10.1145/543434.543435. www.researchgate.net/publication/202165712_Emotion_Design_Attractive_Things_Work_Better

18. Tuch, A., S. Roth, K. Hornbæk, K. Opwis, and J. Bargas-Avila. 2012. "Is Beautiful Really Usable? Toward Understanding the Relation Between Usability, Aaesthetics, and Affect in HCI." *Computers in Human Behavior.* 10.1016/j.chb.2012.03.024 www.researchgate.net/publication/224774619_Is_beautiful_really_usable_Toward_understanding_the_relation_between_usability_aesthetics_and_affect_in_HCI

19. Walter, A. August 2012. "Emotional Interface Design: The Gateway to Passionate Users." *Treehouse.* https://blog.teamtreehouse.com/emotional-interface-design-the-gateway-to-passionate-users

Chapter 6

1. "U.S. Overall Customer Satisfaction." *theacsi.org.* www.theacsi.org/national-economic-indicator/us-overall-customer-satisfaction (accessed on November 09, 2021).

2. Spector, D. May 09, 2014. "These Hilarious Charts Will Show You Exactly Why Correlation Doesn't Mean Causation." *Business Insider.* www.businessinsider.com/spurious-correlations-by-tyler-vigen-2014-5

3. Silverstein, S. December 05, 2014. "6 Compelling Correlations That Make Absolutely No Sense." *Business Insider.* www.businessinsider.com/real-maps-ridiculous-correlations-2014-11

4. Henseler, J., C.M. Ringle, and R.R. Sinkovics. January 2009. "The Use of Partial Least Squares Path Modeling in International Marketing." *Advances in International Marketing,* pp. 277–319. Emerald JAI Press. https://www.researchgate.net/publication/229892421_The_Use_of_Partial_Least_Squares_Path_Modeling_in_International_Marketing

5. Turvill, W. August 01, 2016. "Trinity Mirror Boss: New Day Failed Because Consumers Didn't Want What They Said They Wanted." *CITYA.M.com.* www.cityam.com/trinity-mirror-boss-new-day-newspaper-failed-because/

6. Marion. May 01, 2015. "What to Learn From Tropicana's Packaging Redesign Failure?" *TheBrandingJournal.com.* www.thebrandingjournal.com/2015/05/what-to-learn-from-tropicanas-packaging-redesign-failure/

7. Elliott, S. February 22, 2009. "Tropicana Discovers Some Buyers Are Passionate About Packaging." *The New York Times.* www.nytimes.com/2009/02/23/business/media/23adcol.html?pagewanted=all

8. Zajonc, R.B. December 2001. "Mere Exposure: A Gateway to the Subliminal." *Current Directions in Psychological Science* 10, no. 6, pp. 224–228. doi:10.1111/1467-8721.00154. S2CID 40942173. https://psycnet.apa.org/record/2001-05842-009

9. Young, S., and V. Ciummo. June 16, 2009. "Managing Risk in a Package Redesign: What Can We Learn From Tropicana?" *PackagingStrategies.com.* www.packagingstrategies.com/articles/91264-managing-risk-in-a-package-redesign-what-can-we-learn-from-tropicana

Chapter 7

1. Barrett, L.F. 2004. "Feelings or Words? Understanding the Content in Self-Report Ratings of Experienced Emotion." *Journal of Personality and Social Psychology* 87, no.2, pp. 266–281. www.ncbi.nlm.nih.gov/pmc/articles/PMC1351136/

2. Barrett, L.F. October 1997. "The Relationships Among Momentary Emotion Experiences, Personality Descriptions, and Retrospective Ratings of Emotion." *Personality & Social Psychology Bulletin* 23, no. 10, p. 1100. www.affective-science.org/pubs/1997/FB97.pdf

3. "AI Beats Humans At Emotional Recognition Test In Landmark Study." *Iflscience.com.* www.iflscience.com/technology/ai-beats-humans-emotional-recognition-test-landmark-study/all/ (accessed on November 11, 2021).

4. Graham, J. August 08, 2017. "Walmart Wants to Monitor Shoppers' Facial Expressions." *USA Today.* https://usatoday.com/story/money/2017/08/08/walmart-wants-monitor-shoppers-facial-expressions/550671001/

5. Wakefield, J. October 09, 2014. "Comedy Club Charges Per Laugh with Facial Recognition." *BBC.* www.bbc.com/news/technology-29551380

6. Jurist, E. 2019. "Review of How Emotions Are Made: The Secret Life of the Brain." *Journal of Theoretical and Philosophical Psychology* 39. 10.1037/teo0000098. https://www.researchgate.net/publication/332585981_Review_of_How_Emotions_Are_Made_The_Secret_Life_of_the_Brain

7. Philips, M. March 06, 2017. "Design for Emotion to Increase User Engagement." https://blog.prototypr.io/design-for-emotion-to-increase-user-engagement-3a2560b4b93c

Chapter 8

1. See Hagen, P. 2012.

2. *LinkedIn report.* September 2015. "Rethink the B2B Buyers Journey." https://business.linkedin.com/content/dam/business/marketing-solutions/global/en_US/campaigns/pdfs/rethink-b2b-buyers-journey-v03.09-eng-us.pdf

3. Zak, P.J. July 18, 2019. "How Our Brains Decide When to Trust." *HBR.* The Big Idea Series / Broken Trust. https://hbr.org/2019/07/how-our-brains-decide-when-to-trust

4. Neumann, I.D. April 04, 2007. "Oxytocin: The Neuropeptide of Love Reveals Some of Its Secrets." *Cell Metabolism* 5, no. 4, pp. 231–233. https://www.cell.com/cell-metabolism/comments/S1550-4131(07)00069-1

Chapter 9

1. Gavett, G. April 28, 2014. " Why a Quarter of Americans Don't Trust Their Employers." *HBR.* https://hbr.org/2014/04/why-a-quarter-of-americans-dont-trust-their-employers

2. Zak, P.J. January–February 2017. "The Neuroscience of Trust." *Harvard Business Review*, pp. 84–90. https://hbr.org/2017/01/the-neuroscience-of-trust

3. *Gallup.* 2017. "State of the Global Workplace Report." *Gallup*, p.41. https://fundacionprolongar.org/wp-content/uploads/2019/07/State-of-the-Global-Workplace_Gallup-Report.pdf

4. Robertson-Smith, G., and C. Markwick. 2009. "Employee Engagement: A Review of Current Research and its Implications." *Institute for Employment Studies*, p. 35. https://www.employment-studies.co.uk/system/files/resources/files/469.pdf

5. "The Autobiography of Benjamin Franklin." Archived January 18, 2015, at the Wayback Machine, p. 48. https://www.ushistory.org/franklin/autobiography/page48.htm

6. Melin, A., and M. Egkolfopoulou. June 01, 2021. "Employees Are Quitting Instead of Giving Up Working From Home." *Bloomberg.com.* www.bloomberg.com/news/articles/2021-06-01/return-to-office-employees-are-quitting-instead-of-giving-up-work-from-home

7. Grant, A.M., and F. Gino. 2010. "A Little Thanks Goes a Long Way: Explaining Why Gratitude Expressions Motivate Prosocial Behavior." *Journal of Personality and Social Psychology* 98, no. 6, pp. 946–955. https://www.hbs.edu/faculty/Pages/item.aspx?num=38092

8. Gibson, K.R., K.O'Leary, and J.R. Weintraub. January 23, 2020. "The Little Things That Make Employees Feel Appreciated." *HBR. https://hbr.org/2020/01/the-little-things-that-make-employees-feel-appreciated*

Chapter 10

1. Davey, N. December 06, 2018. "2018's Key Customer Experience Trends—and How They Impacted CX Strategies." *MyCustomer.com.* www.mycustomer.com/experience/engagement/2018s-key-customer-experience-trends-and-how-they-impacted-cx-strategies

2. "U.S. Overall Customer Satisfaction." *theacsi.org.* www.theacsi.org/national-economic-indicator/us-overall-customer-satisfaction (accessed November 09, 2021).

3. Thompson, B. February 07, 2018. "An Inconvenient Truth: 93% of Customer Experience Initiatives are Failing…" *CustomerThink.com.* https://customerthink.com/an-inconvenient-truth-93-of-customer-experience-initiatives-are-failing/

4. Schmidt-Subramanian, M. September 10, 2020. "How To Measure Value For Customer." *Forrester Report.* https://www.forrester.com/report/How-To-Measure-Value-For-Customer/RES162137

5. Author interview with Brown, M.

Chapter 11

1. Murray, P.N., Ph.D. February 26, 2013. "How Emotions Influence What We Buy." *Psychology Today.* www.psychologytoday.com/intl/blog/inside-the-consumer-mind/201302/how-emotions-influence-what-we-buy

2. Chandy, C., and D. Thursby-Pelham. 1993. "Renault Clio: Adding Value in a Recession." In *Advertising Works 7*, C. Baker, ed. Henley-on-Thames. UK: NTC Publications. https://www.warc.com/fulltext/JAR/84600.htm

3. Heath, R., D. Brandt, and A. Nairn. December 2006. "Brand Relationships: Strengthened by Emotion, Weakened by Attention." *Journal of Advertising Research*, pp. 410–419. https://www.warc.com/fulltext/JAR/84600.htm

4. Heath, R., D. Brandt, and A. Nairn. December 2006. "Brand Relationships: Strengthened by Emotion, Weakened by Attention." *Journal of Advertising Research*, pp. 410–419. https://www.warc.com/fulltext/JAR/84600.htm

5. Brandt, D. January 2016. "What's Next: Emotions Give a Lift to Advertising." *Nielsen.* www.nielsen.com/us/en/insights/report/2016/whats-next-emotions-give-a-lift-to-advertising/

6. Seiter, C. March 17, 2014. "How Our Brains Decide What We Share Online." *Fast Company.* www.fastcompany.com/3027699/how-our-brains-decide-what-we-share-online

7. Dooley, R. n.d. "Emotional Ads Work Best." *Neurosciencemarketing.com.* www.neurosciencemarketing.com/blog/articles/emotional-ads-work-best.htm#sthash.yu8l31Jn.dpuf

8. *Advert.* 2021. "Hyundai Driving towards a Sustainable Future." www.youtube.com/watch?v=hRkhOUyQEzQ

9. *Accenture.* 2019. "Accenture Strategy's Global Consumer Pulse Survey 2019." www.accenture.com/_acnmedia/PDF-123/Accenture-COVID19-Pulse-Survey-Research-PoV.pdf

10. "UK Customer Experience Excellence 2020—Meet your New Customer. Competing in the new reality." *KPMG Nunwood Report*, July 2020. https://

assets.kpmg/content/dam/kpmg/im/pdf/kpmg-nunwood-customer-experience-meet-your-new-customer.pdf

11. *5wpr.com.* 2020. "Consumer Culture | 5W Public Relations Report." www.5wpr.com/new/research/consumer-culture-report/

12. *Accenture.* December 05, 2018. "From Me to We: The Rise of the Purpose-Led Brand." www.accenture.com/us-en/insights/strategy/brand-purpose?c=strat_competitiveagilnovalue_10437227&n=mrl_1118

13. Cassidy, F. December 19, 2019. "Mary Portas: Retail is Entering a Brand-New Era." *Racounter.net.* https://www.raconteur.net/retail/mary-portas-retail/?zephr_sso_ott=ws0WWQ

14. *Accenture.* February 20, 2020. "Generation P(urpose): From Fidelity to Future Value." https://www.accenture.com/bg-en/insights/strategy/generation-purpose

15. Cheeseman, G.M. March 13, 2020. "Patagonia to Consumers: Repair and Recycle Your Garments." *TriplePundit.com.* www.triplepundit.com/story/2020/patagonia-consumers-repair-and-recycle-your-garments/86871

16. Beer, J. February 21, 2018. "How Patagonia Grows Every Time It Amplifies Its Social Mission." *Fast Company.*

17. Gibson, k. September 21, 2018. "Colin Kaepernick is Nike's $6 Billion Man." *CBSnews.com.* https://www.cbsnews.com/news/colin-kaepernick-nike-6-billion-man/

18. Sweeney, E. April 19, 2018. "Study: Brands with a Purpose Grow 2x Faster than Others." *Marketing Dive.* www.marketingdive.com/news/study-brands-with-a-purpose-grow-2x-faster-than-others/521693/

19. Walpert-Levy, T. April 2020. "Google Search Data Reveals How Brands Can Help During the Coronavirus Pandemic." *ThinkwithGoogle.com.* www.thinkwithgoogle.com/consumer-insights/consumer-trends/coronavirus-needs/

20. Seiter, C. March 17, 2014. "How Our Brains Decide What We Share Online." *Fast Company.* www.fastcompany.com/3027699/how-our-brains-decide-what-we-share-online

21. Zak, P.J., A.A. Stanton, and S. Ahmadi. 2007. "Oxytocin Increases Generosity in Humans." *PLoS ONE* 2, no. 11, p. e1128. doi:10.1371/journal.pone.000112. https://journals.plos.org/plosone/article?id=10.1371/journal.pone.0001128

22. *Science Daily.* November 16, 2010. "Oxytocin Increases Advertising's Influence: Hormone Heightened Sensitivity to Public Service Announcements." *Society for Neuroscience.* https://www.sciencedaily.com/releases/2010/11/101115160404.htm#:~:text=Oxytocin%20increases%20advertising's%20influence%3A%20Hormone%20heightened%20sensitivity%20to%20public%20service%20announcements,-Date%3A%20November%202016&text=Summary%3A,system%20for%20trust%20and%20empathy

23. Brinker, S. June 23, 2021. "Are CMOs Falling Behind with Martech? The C-Suite Thinks So, and They May Be Right." *Customer Think*. https://customerthink.com/are-cmos-falling-behind-with-martech-the-c-suite-thinks-so-and-they-may-be-right/

Chapter 12

1. Breuer, R., H. Fanderl, N. Maechler, S. Moritz, and F. van der Marel. July 12, 2019. "What Matters in Customer-Experience Transformations." *McKinsey.com* www.mckinsey.com/business-functions/marketing-and-sales/our-insights/what-matters-in-customer-experience-cx-transformations
2. Bucy, M., A. Finlayson, G. Kelly, and C. Moye. May 09, 2016. "The 'How' of Transformation." *McKinsey.com*. www.mckinsey.com/industries/retail/our-insights/the-how-of-transformation#
3. Tabrizi, B., E. Lam, K. Girard, and V. Irvin, March 13, 2019. "Digital Transformation Is Not About Technology." *HBR.com*. https://hbr.org/2019/03/digital-transformation-is-not-about-technology
4. Schmidt-Subramanian, M. September 10, 2020. "How To Measure Value For Customer." *Forrester*. www.forrester.com/report/How+To+Measure+Value+For+Customer/RES162137
5. Davey, N. December 06, 2018. "2018's Key Customer Experience Trends—and How They Impacted CX Strategies." *MyCustomer.com*. www.mycustomer.com/experience/engagement/2018s-key-customer-experience-trends-and-how-they-impacted-cx-strategies
6. Akhtar, O. 2021. "The 2021 State of Digital Transformation." *Altimeter* 202. www.prophet.com/download/the-2021-state-of-digital-transformation/
7. Author Interview with Brown, M. March 17, 2021.
8. Mela, C.F., and B. Cooper. July–August 2021. "Don't Buy the Wrong Marketing Tech." *Harvard Business Review*. https://hbr.org/2021/07/dont-buy-the-wrong-marketing-tech?utm_medium=social&utm_campaign=hbr&utm_source=twitter&tpcc=orgsocial_edit

Chapter 13

1. Du, R.Y., O. Netzer, D.A. Schweidel, and D. Mitra. October 29, 2020. "Capturing Marketing Information to Fuel Growth." *Journal of Marketing*. www.columbia.edu/~on2110/Papers/Du_Netzer_Scweidel_Mitra.pdf
2. *Quantcast.com*. n.d. "Quantcast Helped IKEA Double the Efficiency of Customer Acquisition." *Quantcast Case Study*. www.quantcast.com/case-study/ikea/

3. Moore, A. 2021. "AI-Enabled Contact Center Analytics For Dummies®." NICE Nexidia Special Edition, *John Wiley & Sons, Inc.* www.nice.com/optimizing-customer-engagements/Documents/ai_based_contact_center_analytics_for_dummies.pdf

4. Moore, A. 2021. "AI-Enabled Contact Center Analytics For Dummies®." NICE Nexidia Special Edition, John Wiley & Sons, Inc. www.nice.com/optimizing-customer-engagements/Documents/ai_based_contact_center_analytics_for_dummies.pdf

5. Minkara, O. October 2020. "The ROI of an AI in Modern CX Programs: Happy Customers, Service Excellence, and Financial Success." Aberdeen. www.toolbox.com/marketing/customer-experience/articles/ai-in-customer-experience-cx-in-2021-impact-analysis/

6. "How Customers Think, Feel, And Act: The Paradigm Of Business Outcomes." *A Forrester Consulting Thought Leadership Paper Commissioned By FocusVision*, June 2019. https://cloud.kapostcontent.net/pub/d2a85d5e-c053-4bfc-ae8d-f1a9c0b2af31/whitepaper-how-customers-think-feel-and-act-the-paradigm-of-business-outcomes?kui=MtTZamfFfmzvSS4fnSaD4Q

7. Author Interview with Ten-Pow, J.

Chapter 14

1. Alcántara, A.M. July 27, 2021. "McDonald's Appoints Its First Global Chief Customer Officer." *The Wall Street Journal.* www-wsj-com.cdn.ampproject.org/c/s/www.wsj.com/amp/articles/mcdonalds-appoints-its-first-global-chief-customer-officer-11627406847

2. Amazon Science page on LinkedIn. www.linkedin.com/showcase/amazonscience/ (accessed August 20, 2021).

3. Lunden, I. February 09, 2021. "Symend Nabs $43M for a Platform to Help Customers Avoid Defaulting on Bills." *TechCrunch.com.* https://techcrunch.com/2021/02/09/symend-nabs-43m-for-a-platform-to-help-customers-avoid-defaulting-on-bills/?guccounter=1&guce_referrer=aHR0cHM6Ly93d3cuZ29vZ2xlLmNvbS8&guce_referrer_sig=AQAAAGZfLJY3xMvyNrdMjm9qkvEdaeuvCMZ-4APEuzQt5e__DZw9iJzNIBp76WhsT20eiBHvCKwxo0GctC2IGPn18_dnuSmfXPFxmvZz3-qDV0uDdP8HPqtEOykSDJO8HMKTYPgXP6NlEUFZHxh8J98MgalhMHR2N-rEXwUArxlzi-gD

About the Author

Zhecho Dobrev is a Principal Consultant at Beyond Philosophy, pioneers in the field of Customer Experience, named as one of the top 50 leading consultancies in UK by the Financial Times for the last four years.

For over 13 years as a part of the Beyond Philosophy team, Zhecho has been helping many of the world's most renowned organizations improve their Customer Experience including American Express, FedEx, Heineken and Caterpillar to name a few. Zhecho has covered a large ground, having worked extensively in the US, Canada, UK, Europe, Middle East and East Asia. One of the clients Zhecho worked with as part of the Beyond Philosophy team—Maersk Line, the world's largest container shipping company, improved their net promoter score by 40 points in 30 months, which led to a 10 percent rise in shipping volumes. A recent bank client that Zhecho has been working with went from second in NPS scores to a leader with more than 20 percent gap to the nearest follower.

Over the years, Zhecho has been leading Beyond Philosophy's practice in a number of fields such as conducting advanced customer research and data analysis to uncover subconscious and emotional value drivers, as well as unmet customer needs in the market; helping organizations define their strategy and the experience they want to provide to customers; conducting Journey Mapping projects and applying Behavior Science principles in the redesign the experience, training management and aspiring customer experience professionals on the secrets to managing customer experience and so on. Lately, Zhecho has been exploring the use of more advanced and implicit research techniques such as Facial Emotion Recognition and also the use of AI in organizations.

Zhecho is also a sought-after International Conference Speaker. He has spoken to Senior Executives at conferences to the likes of Caterpillar, Michelin, AT&T, Maersk Line and at International Customer Experience Conferences.

Zhecho has an MBA from the University of Bedfordshire, UK and an MSc in International Relations from the University of Sofia, Bulgaria.

Index

CPSIA information can be obtained
at www.ICGtesting.com
Printed in the USA
BVHW031020100922
R14014500001B/R140145PG646611BVX00005B/5